SILVER APPLES, GOLDEN APPLES

And walk among long dappled grass,
And pluck till time and times are done
The silver apples of the moon,
The golden apples of the sun.

from 'The Song of Wandering Aengus'
W.B. Yeats

SILVER APPLES, GOLDEN APPLES

BEST LOVED IRISH VERSE

CHOSEN BY

FRANK DELANEY

ILLUSTRATED BY

JULIE HAYES

THE
BLACKSTAFF
PRESS
BELFAST AND WOLFEBORO, NEW HAMPSHIRE

First published in 1987 by
The Blackstaff Press Limited
3 Galway Park, Dundonald, Belfast BT16 0AN, Northern Ireland
and
27 South Main Street, Wolfeboro, New Hampshire 03894 USA
with the assistance of
The Arts Council of Northern Ireland

Printed in Northern Ireland by
The Universities Press Limited

British Library Cataloguing in Publication Data
Silver apples, golden apples: best-loved
Irish verse.
1. English poetry — Irish authors
I. Delaney, Frank
821'.008'09415   PR8851

Library of Congress Cataloging-in-Publication Data.
Silver apples, golden apples.
Includes index.
1. English poetry — Irish authors.   2. English poetry —
Translations from Irish.   3. Irish poetry — Translations
into English.   4. Ireland — Poetry.   I. Delaney, Frank,
1942–   .   II. Hayes, Julie, 1965–   .
PR8851.S55   1987   821'.008'089162   87-24296

ISBN 0-85640-391-1

CONTENTS

xi

INTRODUCTION

Some years ago, on a BBC radio programme during which renowned people choose their favourite poetry and prose, I heard Seamus Heaney introduce his choice with the worry that he might be 'robbing the nest'. The phrase comes for sure from a country childhood, from those days when a secret trove of speckled eggs had to be properly respected. If not, the bird would leave the nest, the mystique would end in smithereens.

Point taken: one thing to share odd remembered lines of poetry across a table, or over a drink. Setting out a list, though, suggests something definitive, the one and only selection of poems which have sustained, delighted, stimulated, for years. The assignment, seen from any number of angles, contains obvious risks. Nevertheless, most writers jump at the opportunity to pick their country's all-time greats and the object of my exercise here is to remind, to recollect, to stir old and pleasant embers, to share pleasure.

This anthology is called 'Best-loved' because I believe these poems qualify under that heading among generations of Irish in all the counties. In many ways the compilation, specifically intended to meet popular likings, has chosen itself. Much of it dwells in old school-books, or has called itself out from a half-remembered line here and there, heard perhaps from the lips of someone who, though without much 'book-learning', was pleased to quote it for the music or the romance it contained – 'My thoughts on white ships and the King o' Spain's daughter'.

The range of poems here seems wide enough to need a note of explanation. They came together in a combination of thought and affection – heart, head and memory. If the mixture of feeling and idea coincided at all, in any kind of mutuality, then the history of the Irish and their poetry would also be reflected along the way. Not just the politics, not just the literature; ideas and feelings abound within lines learned by heart in many a schoolroom – countrywide emotion, therefore, recollected in tranquillity. It matters not what order the poems cluster into, chronological, or regional, or thematic – the messages remain constant. They include the famous fascination with nature, moody whispers of the mystic Celtic heritage, the sacrificial and adoring poems of Christianity. They are concerned with war, death, loss, sadness, melancholy and blood-red resistance, north and south and east and west. They embody satire, wild humour, love, chance, legend – life itself.

I have to say that I began to compile the book moved by love and enjoyment, and absolutely certain that in this attitude I was not alone. Irish people, formally educated or not, have a gift for poems, either making or saying them. Go backwards in time, and all along the way the poem figures in real terms, not in any ethereal or compartmentalised role, but in the ordinary rut and whistle of every day. It was a means of taunting or dismissing an enemy or mocking an inhospitable neighbour, a way of praising a friend or calling over a girl, a formal method of flattering a chieftain or asking for favour. It has modern political implications too – the 1916 insurrection in Dublin became known as the 'Poets' Rising', due to the fact that before the event many of the leaders had used poetry as a means of addressing and conveying their own political aspirations.

Verses turned up in all kinds of earth. Some belonged in families, from thumbed and inherited collections. Many were recited during that broadcasting benchmark, *Ballad-makers' Saturday Night* on Radio Eireann. One popular publication, *Ireland's Own,* continues in the tradition of publishing ballads and monologues and still achieves good sales at home and abroad.

In the higher realms, among the technocracy of poetry, where metre, prosody and legislated composition reign, such party pieces do not, of course, register on the scale: they were no more than rhyming entertainments, handy for carrying light loads of nostalgia, local heroism, quirkiness, or mystery. Some were sung: 'Good men and true in this house who dwell'; sentiment ran riot, and the reach was towards a lower common

xvi

denominator of emotion than is accepted today in respect of the literary word 'poem'.

Decry their parochial flavours and concerns at your peril; read Patrick Kavanagh's 'Epic': Homer '. . . made the Iliad from such/A local row.' These old ballads and the means of using them for entertainment came from a long and vivid oral tradition where the shape of the words rolling out of the mouth, and the tune of the rhyme in the dancehall of the mind, and the easy satisfaction in their natural sturdiness, compensated for many pains and eased many more. The music goes on. I still enjoy the memory of encountering this rhyming balladry when I worked, in summer holidays, for a local farmer in his hayfield. I still remember being surprised at him and his hired labour. All of them had quit school at the first legally permissible moment, that is to say at fourteen years of age; nonetheless, they were able to jingle out lines like 'It was the schooner *Hesperus*/That sailed the wintry sea'. These men may not have known or appreciated poetry in any academic or literary sense, yet it belonged to them in small daily ways, like their penknives or their pocket watches – natural, personal, undramatised possessions.

An ancient system had bequeathed them this awareness, a system which always enshrined poetry, a system not unlike that which connects classical music to folk tune. Formal poetry, with a rigorous intellectual base, wove a major strand of Ireland's culture. Before the dark days of forbidden education, back further through the sad realisation that their earls had fled, before the unsuccessful Elizabethan genocide was attempted, and before that again, in the days of the saints and scholars, the island of Ireland virtually counted as a poem in itself. The history began as myth, was reconstructed as poem, and in words that were joined according to strict rules by bards and journeymen and court musicians, the shape and soul of the country was defined. In the same way as cousins in the foothills of the Himalayas told – and still tell – their long, neighbourly and courtly stories, the early inhabitants had relied on narrative, on an oral communication, to forge, as a later star,

James Joyce, put it, 'the uncreated conscience' of their race.

Poems of intellectual discipline never arrived as lightly as the ballads. Grace and deep thought became principal requirements, the poet reflected upon the seen and unseen forces of world and spirit, and then reflected them onwards. The task was performed to the highest rigour, but always taking account of that primary requirement summed up in Matthew Arnold's words, 'genuine poetry is conceived and composed in the soul'.

The record of Irish poetry becomes even more astonishing when you consider how great a tide it had to struggle against. Not the tide of history or oppression or famine or defeat or loss or exile – all of these matters produce essential poetry. The tide of language flowed against the country in a far more serious and fundamental way. The poets' own language – the very tooling of their work – was outlawed, and in time the poems had to change mode, be expressed in a foreign tongue, English. Did the poetry miss any strides in the effort? Undountedly the heart of a nation beats closer and warmer in national tongue, but in English so many Irish poets forged such beauty that one sometimes wonders whether the forced change of language did not throw up some new vitality, some added dimension.

In essence, then, the country never lacked poetry, in whatever form. Monkish scribes and learned barbs crafted exquisite pieces of mannered poetry; countrymen created valid balladry; the figure of the poet, from the earliest times, carried authority and stature and learning. The development of the island, of the mores, the society, the ruling structures, the preoccupations, could – can – all be traced in this, the longest surviving member of the composing arts. Whether the record was made self-consciously by those who felt that poetry was a duty, or whether it wrote itself down out of spiritual impulse, made no difference – the fact was the poetry and the poetry was the fact, and this selection, I hope, provides a sturdy tranche of evidence.

The period of the anthology ranges from the earliest times to Louis MacNeice. In the interests of familiarity, I have also included many poems whose popularity outflanks their excellence, who must belong far more to the ballad, or even more colloquial tradition, than to poetry in the technocratic sense. They come from all over Ireland, regardless of creed or county. They take account, therefore, of the various traditions on which poetry fed – from the dominant Christianity of the early days, to the enforced abstract patriotism of Dark Rosaleen's political wilderness, to the rural melancholy or earthy good will of farmers and drovers. Their composers were monastic or Protestant or polished or uneducated or jewellers or rawboned or bereft women or fighting men. They tell long stories of long, long traditions – battling for survival against an annihilating neighbour, looking back to a heroic past, using myth as a fountain, recording passion, arriving sharp-edged and up to date with the likes of Kavanagh, MacNeice and Austin Clarke who did not so much don the mantle of Yeats, as insist upon wearing their own clothes. Above all, these poems demonstrate an Irish poetic temperament without distancing it from its roots.

It is impossible to be definitive in something as subjective as personal choice. Things as ephemeral as the mood of the moment may even have a bearing: as anybody who has ever judged a literary competition will agree, at another time, in another place, a different collection would emerge. Even now I twitch at the thought of a poem I might have passed by; I shall twitch again and again. Which of Yeats's should be included – how many dozens therefore do I have to leave out? Have I done justice to Ferguson, that valiant Ulsterman who tried, with poetry, to bridge the gap between the Anglo-Irish and the rest of the island? Has the tradition of the original Gaelic been fully reflected? These and a hundred other questions attack anyone whose enthusiasms lead him in the direction of such an anthology. Blame the enthusiasm – most of the blunders are 'blunders of the heart'. Nor will I have the luxury of knowing, as with, say, the writing of ordinary prose, that only I alone know what has had to be excluded. My defence will be that a rough count of the possibilities for an anthology of Irish poetry which could please absolutely everybody, would render publication almost impossible, or at least economically ridiculous.

The sheer size of the book would dismiss several acres of forest.

In Cork not long ago there lived a sculptor and stonemason called Seamus Murphy — he died in 1975 — who wrote one of the most influential and seminal books ever to come out of Ireland, *Stone Mad*. It describes his life and his attitude to his life, and in these matters he had a true artist's wisdom, that is to say, his perceptions may be applied universally, without any regard for boundaries of geography or time. One of his observations seems appropriate to this book, and especially — bearing in mind the story they collectively tell — to the poets whose work created it. He wrote, 'With hammer, mallet and chisel we have shaped and fashioned rough boulders. We often curse our material and often we speak kindly to it. . . We try to impose ourselves on it, but if we know our material and respect it we will often take a suggestion from it, and our work will be the better for it.' May you read this anthology of poems in this spirit also.

FRANK DELANEY
London, Autumn 1987

THE FAIRIES

Up the airy mountain,
   Down the rushy glen,
We daren't go a-hunting
   For fear of little men;
Wee folk, good folk,
   Trooping all together;
Green jacket, red cap,
   And white owl's feather!

Down along the rocky shore
   Some make their home,
They live on crispy pancakes
   Of yellow tide-foam;
Some in the reeds
   Of the black mountain-lake,
With frogs for their watch-dogs,
   All night awake.

High on the hill-top
   The old King sits;
He is now so old and grey
   He's nigh lost his wits.
With a bridge of white mist
   Columbkill he crosses,
On his stately journeys
   From Slieveleague to Rosses;
Or going up with music,
   On cold starry nights,
To sup with the Queen
   Of the gay Northern Lights.

They stole little Bridget
   For seven years long;
When she came down again
   Her friends were all gone.

They took her lightly back,
 Between the night and morrow;
They thought that she was fast asleep,
 But she was dead with sorrow.
They have kept her ever since
 Deep within the lake,
On a bed of flag-leaves,
 Watching till she wake.

By the craggy hill-side,
 Through the mosses bare,
They have planted thorn-trees
 For pleasure here and there.
Is any man so daring
 As dig them up in spite?
He shall find their sharpest thorns
 In his bed at night.

Up the airy mountain
 Down the rushy glen,
We daren't go a-hunting,
 For fear of little men;
Wee folk, good folk,
 Trooping all together;
Green jacket, red cap,
 And white owl's feather!

WILLIAM ALLINGHAM

FOUR DUCKS ON A POND

Four ducks on a pond,
A grass bank beyond,
A blue sky of spring,
White birds on the wing:
What a little thing
To remember for years —
To remember with tears!

WILLIAM ALLINGHAM

JOHNNY, I HARDLY KNEW YE

While going the road to sweet Athy,
    Hurroo! hurroo!
While going the road to sweet Athy,
    Hurroo! hurroo!
While going the road to sweet Athy,
A stick in my hand and a drop in my eye,
A doleful damsel I heard cry:
'Och, Johnny, I hardly knew ye.
With drums and guns, and guns and drums,
    The enemy nearly slew ye,
    My darling dear, you look so queer,
Och, Johnny, I hardly knew ye!

'Where are your eyes that looked so mild?
    Hurroo! hurroo!
Where are your eyes that looked so mild?
    Hurroo! hurroo!
Where are your eyes that looked so mild,
When my poor heart you first beguiled?
Why did you run from me and the child?
    Och, Johnny, I hardly knew ye!
With drums, etc.

'Where are the legs with which you run?
    Hurroo! hurroo!
Where are the legs with which you run?
    Hurroo! hurroo!
Where are the legs with which you run,
When you went to carry a gun? –
Indeed, your dancing days are done!
    Och, Johnny, I hardly knew ye!
With your drums, etc.

'It grieved my heart to see you sail,
    Hurroo! hurroo!

It grieved my heart to see you sail,
   Hurroo! hurroo!
It grieved my heart to see you sail,
Though from my heart you took leg bail —
Like a cod you're doubled up head and tail.
   Och, Johnny, I hardly knew ye!
With drums, etc.

'You haven't an arm and you haven't a leg,
   Hurroo! hurroo!
You haven't an arm and you haven't a leg,
   Hurroo! hurroo!
You haven't an arm and you haven't a leg,
You're an eyeless, noseless, chickenless egg;
You'll have to be put in a bowl to beg:
   Och, Johnny, I hardly knew ye!
With drums, etc.

'I'm happy for to see you home,
   Hurroo! hurroo!
I'm happy for to see you home,
   Hurroo! hurroo!
I'm happy for to see you home,
All from the island of Sulloon,
So low in flesh, so high in bone,
   Och, Johnny, I hardly knew ye!
With drums, etc.

'But sad as it is to see you so,
   Hurroo! hurroo!
But sad as it is to see you so,
   Hurroo! hurroo!
But sad as it is to see you so,
And to think of you now as an object of woe.
Your Peggy'll still keep ye on as her beau;

Och, Johnny, I hardly knew ye!
With drums and guns, and guns and drums,
    The enemy nearly slew ye,
    My darling dear, you look so queer,
Och, Johnny, I hardly knew ye!'

ANONYMOUS

I AM OF IRELAND

Icham of Irlaunde
Ant of the holy londe of irlande
Gode sir pray ich ye
for of saynte charite,
come ant daunce wyt me,
in irlaunde.

ANONYMOUS

THE NIGHT BEFORE LARRY WAS STRETCHED

The night before Larry was stretched,
The boys they all paid him a visit;
A bait in their sacks, too, they fetched;
They sweated their duds till they riz it:
For Larry was ever the lad,
When a boy was condemned to the squeezer,
Would fence all the duds that he had
To help a poor friend to a sneezer,
And warm his gob 'fore he died.

The boys they came crowding in fast,
They drew all their stools round about him,
Six glims round his trap-case were placed,
He couldn't be well waked without 'em.
When one of us asked could he die
Without having truly repented,
Says Larry, 'That's all in my eye;
And first by the clargy invented,
To get a fat bit for themselves.'

'I'm sorry, dear Larry,' says I,
'To see you in this situation;
And blister my limbs if I lie,
I'd as lieve it had been my own station.'
'Ochone! it's all over,' says he,
'For the neck-cloth I'll be forced to put on,
And by this time tomorrow you'll see
Your poor Larry as dead as a mutton,
Because, why, his courage was good.

'And I'll be cut up like a pie,
And my nob from my body be parted.'
'You're in the wrong box, then,' says I,
'For blast me if they're so hard-hearted;
A chalk on the back of your neck

Is all that Jack Ketch dares to give you;
Then mind not such trifles a feck,
For why should the likes of them grieve you?
And now, boys, come tip us the deck.'

The cards being called for, they played,
Till Larry found one of them cheated;
A dart at his napper he made
(The boy being easily heated);
'Oh, by the hokey, you thief,
I'll scuttle your nob with my daddle!
You cheat me because I'm in grief,
But soon I'll demolish your noddle,
And leave you your claret to drink.'

Then the clergy came in with his book,
He spoke him so smooth and so civil;
Larry tipped him a Kilmainham look,
And pitched his big wig to the devil;
Then sighing, he threw back his head,
To get a sweet drop of the bottle,
And pitiful sighing, he said:
'Oh, the hemp will be soon round my throttle,
And choke my poor windpipe to death.

'Though sure it's the best way to die,
Oh, the devil a better a-living!
For, sure when the gallows is high
Your journey is shorter to heaven:
But what harasses Larry the most,
And makes his poor soul melancholy,
Is to think on the time when his ghost
Will come in a sheet to sweet Molly –
Oh, sure it will kill her alive!'

So moving these last words he spoke,
We all vented our tears in a shower;
For my part, I thought my heart broke,
To see him cut down like a flower.
On his travels we watched him next day,
Oh, the throttler! I thought I could kill him;
But Larry not one word did say,
Nor changed till he came to 'King William' —
Then, musha! his colour grew white.

When he came to the nubbling chit,
He was tucked up so neat and so pretty,
The rumbler jogged off from his feet,
And he died with his feet to the city;
He kicked, too — but that was all pride,
But soon you might see 'twas all over;
Soon after the noose was untied.
And at darky we waked him in clover,
And sent him to take a ground sweat.

ANONYMOUS

9

MY LAGAN LOVE

Where Lagan stream sings lullaby,
   There blows a lily fair.
The twilight is in her eye,
   The night is on her hair.
And, like a lovesick *leanan-sidhe*,
   She hath my heart in thrall.
Nor life I own, nor liberty,
   For love is lord of all.

And often when the beetle's horn
   Hath lulled the eve to sleep;
I steal unto her shieling lorn,
   And thro' the dooring peep.
There in the crickets' singing-stone
   She stirs the bogwood fire,
And hums in sad sweet undertone,
   The song of heart's desire.

Her welcome, like her love for me,
   Is from the heart within;
Her warm kiss is felicity,
   That knows no taint or sin,
When she was only fairly small
   Her gentle mother died,
But true love keeps her memory warm
   By Lagan's silver side.

JOSEPH CAMPBELL

THE STRAYING STUDENT

On a holy day when sails were blowing southward,
A bishop sang the Mass at Inishmore,
Men took one side, their wives were on the other
But I heard the woman coming from the shore:
And wild in despair my parents cried aloud
For they saw the vision draw me to the doorway.

Long had she lived in Rome when Popes were bad,
The wealth of every age she makes her own,
Yet smiled on me in eager admiration,
And for a summer taught me all I know,
Banishing shame with her great laugh that rang
As if a pillar caught it back alone.

I learned the prouder counsel of her throat,
My mind was growing bold as light in Greece;
And when in sleep her stirring limbs were shown,
I blessed the noonday rock that knew no tree:
And for an hour the mountain was her throne,
Although her eyes were bright with mockery.

They say I was sent back from Salamanca
And failed in logic, but I wrote her praise
Nine times upon a college wall in France.
She laid her hand at darkfall on my page
That I might read the heavens in a glance
And I knew every star the Moors have named.

Awake or in my sleep, I have no peace now,
Before the ball is struck, my breath has gone,
And yet I tremble lest she may deceive me
And leave me in this land, where every woman's son
Must carry his own coffin and believe,
In dread, all that the clergy teach the young.

AUSTIN CLARKE

THE LOST HEIFER

When the black herds of the rain were grazing
In the gap of the pure cold wind
And the watery haze of the hazel
Brought her into my mind,
I thought of the last honey by the water
That no hive can find.

Brightness was drenching through the branches
When she wandered again,
Turning the silver out of dark grasses
Where the skylark had lain,
And her voice coming softly over the meadow
Was the mist becoming rain.

AUSTIN CLARKE

PENAL LAW

Burn Ovid with the rest. Lovers will find
A hedge-school for themselves and learn by heart
All that the clergy banish from the mind,
When hands are joined and head bows in the dark.

AUSTIN CLARKE

A DROVER

To Meath of the pastures,
   From wet hills by the sea,
Through Leitrim and Longford
   Go my cattle and me.

I hear in the darkness
   Their slipping and breathing.
I name them the bye-ways
   They're to pass without heeding.

Then the wet, winding roads,
   Brown bogs with black water;
And my thoughts on white ships
   And the King o' Spain's daughter.

O farmer, strong farmer!
   You can spend at the fair,
But your face you must turn
   To your crops and your care.

And soldiers, red soldiers!
   You've seen many lands;
But you walk two and two,
   And by captain's commands.

O the smell of the beasts,
   The wet wind in the morn,
And the proud and hard earth
   Never broken for corn!

And the crowds at the fair,
   The herds loosened and blind,
Loud words and dark faces
   And the wild blood behind.

(O strong men with your best
    I would strive breast to breast
I could quiet your herds
    With my words, with my words!)

I will bring you, my kine,
    Where there's grass to the knee;
But you'll think of scant croppings
    Harsh with salt of the sea.

PADRAIC COLUM

AN OLD WOMAN OF THE ROADS

O, to have a little house!
To own the hearth and stool and all!
The heaped up sods against the fire,
The pile of turf against the wall!

To have a clock with weights and chains
And pendulum swinging up and down!
A dresser filled with shining delph,
Speckled and white and blue and brown!

I could be busy all the day
Clearing and sweeping hearth and floor,
And fixing on their shelf again
My white and blue speckled store!

I could be quiet there at night
Beside the fire and by myself,
Sure of a bed and loth to leave
The ticking clock and the shining delph!

Och! but I'm weary of mist and dark,
And roads where there's never a house nor bush,
And tired I am of bog and road,
And the crying wind and the lonesome hush!

And I am praying to God on high,
And I am praying Him night and day,
For a little house — a house of my own —
Out of the wind's and the rain's way.

PADRAIC COLUM

SHE MOVED THROUGH THE FAIR

My young love said to me, 'My brothers won't mind,
And my parents won't slight you for your lack of kind.'
Then she stepped away from me, and this she did say,
'It will not be long, love, till our wedding day.'

She stepped away from me and she moved through the fair,
And fondly I watched her go here and go there,
Then she went her way homeward with one star awake,
As the swan in the evening moves over the lake.

The people were saying no two were e'er wed
But one had a sorrow that never was said,
And I smiled as she passed with her goods and her gear,
And that was the last that I saw of my dear.

I dreamt it last night that my young love came in,
So softly she entered, her feet made no din;
She came close beside me, and this she did say,
'It will not be long, love, till our wedding day.'

PADRAIC COLUM

O WOMAN, SHAPELY AS THE SWAN

O woman, shapely as the swan,
On your account I shall not die:
The men you've slain – a trivial clan –
Were less than I.

I ask me shall I die for these –
For blossom teeth and scarlet lips –
And shall that delicate swan-shape
Bring me eclipse?

Well-shaped the breasts and smooth the skin,
The cheeks are fair, the tresses free –
And yet I shall not suffer death,
God over me!

Those even brows, that hair like gold,
Those languorous tones, that virgin way,
The flowing limbs, the rounded heel
Slight men betray!

Thy spirit keen through radiant mien,
Thy shining throat and smiling eye,
Thy little palm, thy side like foam –
I cannot die!

O woman, shapely as the swan
In a cunning house hard-reared was I:
O bosom white, O well-shaped palm,
I shall not die!

ANONYMOUS
translated by Padraic Colum

19

BALLAD TO A TRADITIONAL REFRAIN

Red brick in the suburbs, white horse on the wall,
Eyetalian marbles in the City Hall:
O stranger from England, why stand so aghast?
May the Lord in His mercy be kind to Belfast.

This jewel that houses our hopes and our fears
Was knocked up from the swamp in the last hundred years;
But the last shall be first and the first shall be last:
May the Lord in His mercy be kind to Belfast.

We swore by King William there'd never be seen
An All-Irish Parliament at College Green,
So at Stormont we're nailing the flag to the mast:
May the Lord in His mercy be kind to Belfast.

O the bricks they will bleed and the rain it will weep,
And the damp Lagan fog lull the city to sleep;
It's to hell with the future and live on the past:
May the Lord in His mercy be kind to Belfast.

MAURICE JAMES CRAIG

THE MONKS OF THE SCREW

When St Patrick this order established,
    He called us the 'Monks of the Screw';
Good rules he revealed to our Abbot
    To guide us in what we should do.
But first he replenished our fountain
    With liquor the best from on high;
And he said, on the word of a saint,
    That the fountain should never run dry.

'Each year, when your octaves approach,
    In full chapter convened let me find you;
And when to the convent you come,
    Leave your favourite temptation behind you.
And be not a glass in your convent –
    Unless on a festival – found;
And, this rule to enforce, I ordain it
    One festival all the year round.

'My brethren, be chaste – till you're tempted;
    While sober, be grave and discreet;
And humble your bodies with fasting,
    As oft as you've nothing to eat.
Yet, in honour of fasting, one lean face
    Among you I'd always require;
If the Abbot should please, he may wear it,
    If not, let it come to the Prior.'

Come, let each take his chalice, my brethren,
    And with due devotion prepare,
With hands and with voices uplifted,
    Our hymn to conclude with a prayer.

May this chapter oft joyously meet,
  And this gladsome libation renew,
To the Saint, and the Founder, and Abbot,
  And Prior, and Monks of the Screw!

JOHN PHILPOT CURRAN

LAMENT FOR THE DEATH OF EOGHAN RUADH O'NEILL

'Did they dare – did they dare, to slay Owen Roe O'Neill?'
'Yes, they slew with poison him they feared to meet with steel.'
'May God wither up their hearts! May their blood cease to
    flow!
May they walk in living death who poisoned Owen Roe!

'Though it break my heart to hear, say again the bitter words.'
'From Derry, against Cromwell, he marched to measure
    swords;
But the weapon of the Sassanach met him on his way.
And he died at Cloch Uachtar upon St Leonard's Day.

'Wail, wail ye for the Mighty One! Wail, wail, ye for the Dead!
Quench the hearth, and hold the breath – with ashes strew the
    head.
How tenderly we loved him! How deeply we deplore!
Holy Saviour! but to think we shall never see him more!

'Sagest in the council was he, kindest in the hall:
Sure, we never won a battle – 'twas Owen won them all.
Had he lived – had he lived, our dear country had been free;
But he's dead – but he's dead, and 'tis slaves we'll ever be.

'O'Farrell and Clanrickarde, Preston and Red Hugh,
Audley and MacMahon, ye are valiant, wise, and true;
But what – what are ye all to our darling who is gone?
The Rudder of our ship was he – our Castle's corner-stone!

'Wail, wail him through the island! Weep, weep for our pride!
Would that on the battlefield our gallant chief had died!
Weep the victor of Beinn Burb – weep him, young men and old!
Weep for him, ye women – your Beautiful lies cold!

'We thought you would not die – we were sure you would
    not go,
And leave us in our utmost need to Cromwell's cruel blow –
Sheep without a shepherd, when the snow shuts out the sky –
Oh! why did you leave us, Owen? Why did you die?

'Soft as woman's was your voice, O'Neill! Bright was your eye.
Oh! why did you leave us, Owen? Why did you die?
Your troubles are all over; you're at rest with God on high:
But we're slaves, and we're orphans, Owen! Why did you die?'

THOMAS DAVIS

LAMENT OF THE IRISH EMIGRANT

I'm sittin' on the stile, Mary,
    Where we sat side by side
On a bright May mornin', long ago,
    When first you were my bride:
The corn was springin' fresh and green,
    And the lark sang loud and high –
And the red was on your lip, Mary,
    And the love-light in your eye.

The place is little changed, Mary,
    The day is bright as then,
The lark's loud song is in my ear,
    And the corn is green again;
But I miss the soft clasp of your hand,
    And your breath, warm on my cheek,
And I still keep list'nin' for the words
    You never more will speak.

'Tis but a step down yonder lane,
    And the little church stands near –
The church where we were wed, Mary,
    I see the spire from here.
But the graveyard lies between, Mary,
    And my step might break your rest –
For I've laid you, darling! down to sleep,
    With your baby on your breast.

I'm very lonely now, Mary,
    For the poor make no new friends;
But, oh! they love the better still,
    The few our Father sends!
And you were all I had, Mary,
    My blessin' and my pride!
There's nothin' left to care for now,
    Since my poor Mary died.

Yours was the good, brave heart, Mary,
    That still kept hoping on,
When the trust in God had left my soul,
    And my arm's young strength was gone;
There was comfort ever on your lip,
    And the kind look on your brow –
I bless you, Mary, for that same,
    Though you cannot hear me now.

I thank you for the patient smile
    When your heart was fit to break,
When the hunger pain was gnawin' there,
    And you hid it for my sake;
I bless you for the pleasant word,
    When your heart was sad and sore –
Oh! I'm thankful you are gone, Mary,
    Where grief can't reach you more!

I'm biddin' you a long farewell,
    My Mary – kind and true!
But I'll not forget you, darlin,
    In the land I'm goin' to:
They say there's bread and work for all,
    And the sun shines always there –
But I'll not forget old Ireland,
    Were it fifty times as fair!

And often in those grand old woods
    I'll sit and shut my eyes,
And my heart will travel back again
    To the place where Mary lies;

And I'll think I see the little stile
　　Where we sat side by side,
And the springin' corn, and the bright May morn,
　　When first you were my bride.

LADY DUFFERIN

DEIRDRE'S LAMENT FOR THE SONS OF USNACH

The lions of the hill are gone,
And I am left alone – alone –
Dig the grave both wide and deep,
For I am sick, and fain would sleep!

The falcons of the wood are flown,
And I am left alone – alone –
Dig the grave both deep and wide,
And let us slumber side by side.

The dragons of the rock are sleeping,
Sleep that wakes not for our weeping:
Dig the grave and make it ready;
Lay me on my true Love's body.

Lay their spears and bucklers bright
By the warriors' sides aright;
Many a day the Three before me
On their linkèd bucklers bore me.

Lay upon the low grave floor,
'Neath each head, the blue claymore;
Many a time the noble Three
Redden'd those blue blades for me.

Lay the collars, as is meet,
Of their greyhounds at their feet;
Many a time for me have they
Brought the tall red deer to bay.

Oh! to hear my true Love singing,
Sweet as sound of trumpets ringing:
Like the sway of ocean swelling
Roll'd his deep voice round our dwelling.

Oh! to hear the echoes pealing
Round our green and fairy sheeling,
When the Three, with soaring chorus,
Pass'd the silent skylark o'er us.

Echo now, sleep, morn and even –
Lark alone enchant the heaven! –
Ardan's lips are scant of breath, –
Neesa's tongue is cold in death.

Stag, exult on glen and mountain –
Salmon, leap from loch to fountain –
Heron, in the free air warm ye –
Usnach's Sons no more will harm ye!

Erin's stay no more you are,
Rulers of the ridge of war;
Never more 'twill be your fate
To keep the beam of battle straight.

Woe is me! by fraud and wrong –
Traitors false and tyrants strong –
Fell Clan Usnach, bought and sold,
For Barach's feast and Conor's gold!

Woe to Eman, roof and wall! –
Woe to Red Branch, hearth and hall! –
Tenfold woe and black dishonour
To the false and foul Clan Conor!

Dig the grave both wide and deep,
Sick I am, and fain would sleep!
Dig the grave and make it ready,
Lay me on my true Love's body.

ANONYMOUS
translated by Samuel Ferguson

LAMENT FOR THE DEATH OF THOMAS DAVIS

I walked through Ballinderry in the springtime,
  When the bud was on the tree,
And I said, in every fresh-ploughed field beholding
  The sowers striding free,
Scattering broadcast for the corn in golden plenty,
  On the quick, seed-clasping soil,
Even such this day among the fresh-stirred hearts of Erin
  Thomas Davis, is thy toil!

I sat by Ballyshannon in the summer,
  And saw the salmon leap,
And I said, as I beheld the gallant creatures
  Spring glittering from the deep,
Through the spray and through the prone heaps
    striving onward
  To the calm, clear streams above,
So seekest thou thy native founts of freedom, Thomas Davis,
  In thy brightness of strength and love!

I stood on Derrybawn in the autumn,
  I heard the eagle call,
With a clangorous cry of wrath and lamentation
  That filled the wide mountain hall,
O'er the bare, deserted place of his plundered eyrie,
  And I said, as he screamed and soared,
So callest thou, thou wrathful-soaring Thomas Davis,
  For a nation's rights restored.

Young husbandman of Erin's fruitful seed-time,
  In the fresh track of danger's plough!
Who will walk the heavy, toilsome, perilous furrow,
  Girt with freedom's seed-sheets now?
Who will banish with the wholesome crop of knowledge
  The flaunting weed and the bitter thorn,

Now that thou thyself art but a seed for hopeful planting
    Against the resurrection morn?

Young salmon of the flood-time of freedom
    That swells round Erin's shore
Thou wilt leap against their loud, oppressive torrents
    Of bigotry and hate no more!
Drawn downward by their prone material instinct,
    Let them thunder on their rocks, and foam;
Thou hast leaped, aspiring soul, to founts beyond their raging,
    Where troubled waters never come.

But I grieve not, eagle of the empty eyrie,
    That thy wrathful cry is still,
And that the songs alone of peaceful mourners
    Are heard to-day on Erin's hill.
Better far if brothers' wars are destined for us –
    God avert that horrid day, I pray! –
That ere our hands be stained with slaughter fratricidal,
    Thy warm heart should be cold in clay.

But my trust is strong in God who made us brothers,
    That He will not suffer these right hands,
Which thou hast joined in holier rites than wedlock,
    To draw opposing brands.
O many a tuneful tongue that thou madest vocal,
    Would lie cold and silent then,
And songless long once more should often-widowed Erin
    Mourn the loss of her brave young men.

O brave young men, my love, my pride, my promise,
    'Tis on you my hopes are set,
In manliness, in kindliness, in justice,
    To make Erin a nation yet;

Self-respecting, self-relying, self-advancing,
   In union or in severance, free and strong,
And if God grant this, then, under God, to Thomas Davis
   Let the greater praise belong!

SAMUEL FERGUSON

THE LARK IN THE CLEAR AIR

Dear thoughts are in my mind
And my soul soars enchanted,
As I hear the sweet lark sing
In the clear air of the day.
For a tender beaming smile
To my hope has been granted,
And tomorrow she shall hear
All my fond heart would say.

I shall tell her all my love,
All my soul's adoration;
And I think she will hear me
And will not say me nay.
It is this that fills my soul
With its joyous elation,
As I hear the sweet lark sing
In the clear air of the day.

SAMUEL FERGUSON

THE STUDENT AND HIS CAT

I and Pangur Bán, my cat,
'Tis a like task we are at;
Hunting mice is his delight,
Hunting words I sit all night.

Better far than praise of men
'Tis to sit with book and pen;
Pangur bears me no ill-will,
He, too, plies his simple skill.

'Tis a merry thing to see
At our tasks how glad are we,
When at home we sit and find
Entertainment to our mind.

Oftentimes a mouse will stray
In the hero Pangur's way;
Oftentimes my keen thought set
Takes a meaning in its net.

'Gainst the wall he sets his eye
Full and fierce and sharp and sly;
'Gainst the wall of knowledge I
All my little wisdom try.

When a mouse darts from its den,
O! how glad is Pangur then;
O! what gladness do I prove
When I solve the doubts I love.

So in peace our task we ply,
Pangur Bán, my cat, and I;
In our arts we find our bliss,
I have mine, and he has his.

Practice every day has made
Pangur perfect in his trade;
I get wisdom day and night,
Turning darkness into light.

ANONYMOUS
translated by Robin Flower

AN IRISH MOTHER

A wee slip drawin' water,
   Me ould man at the plough.
No grown-up son nor daughter,
   That's the way we're farmin' now,
'No work and little pleasure'
   Was the cry before they wint.
Now they're gettin' both full measure,
   So I ought to be contint.

Great wages men is givin'
   In that land beyant the say,
But 'tis lonely, lonely living
   Whin the childher is away.

Och, the baby in the cradle,
   Blue eyes and curlin' hair,
God knows I'd give a gra'dle
   To have little Pether there;
No doubt he'd find it funny
   Lyin' here upon me arm,
Him – that's earnin' the good money,
   On a Californy farm.

Six pounds it was or sivin
   He sint last quarter day,
But 'tis lonely, lonely livin'
   Whin the childher is away.

God is good – no better,
   And the Divil might be worse,
Each month there comes a letther
   Bringing somethin' for the purse.
And me ould man's heart rejoices
   Whin he reads they're doin' fine,

But it's oh! to hear their voices,
  And to feel their hands in mine.

To see the cattle drivin'
  And the young ones makin' hay,
'Tis a lonely land to live in
  Whin the childher is away.

Whin the shadows do be fallin'
  On the ould man there an' me,
'Tis hard to keep from callin'
  'Come in, childher, to yer tea!'
I can almost hear them comin'
  Mary Kate and little Con –
Och! but I'm the foolish woman,
  Sure they're all grown up an' gone.

That their sins may be forgiven,
  And not wan go astray,
I doubt I'd stay in Heaven
  If them childher was away.

PERCY FRENCH

I'm a judge in Boston city, I've a countless hoard of
    dollars;
  I go northward in the summer, I go southward in the
    snow.
I've the smartest fur-trimmed overcoats, the whitest linen
    collars,
I enjoy the best society with Presidents and scholars,
  And the people shout 'God bless him' as I go.

The lawyers call me Solomon, the merchants call me
    Croesus:
  I'm 'most affable' to journalists when I am interviewed:
I can never pass the fashionable, photo-selling places,
But I'm smilingly confronted by my daughters' pretty faces
  They're exhibited in every attitude.

There's a queenly, quiet lady who is hostess at my table,
  Who is mistress of my household, who is mother of my
    girls.
(Gentle wife!) she dresses finer than the princess in a fable,
Oh, the shimmer of her satin and the richness of her sable!
  Oh, the glory of her diamonds and her pearls!

I have all that man can wish for, I am honoured and
    respected
  By the highest and the lowest, by the freeman and the
    slave.
They put me down Vice-President for each new work
    projected,
For next session of the Congress I am sure to be elected —
  Oh, my lost green land, my land beyond the wave!

Perhaps my eyes are age-dimmed, but I think that dawn
    was whiter
    Over Connemara's mountains than behind that eastern
    range;

On the grey grass the young lark sang, with no human
to affright her,
Yea, in Connemara's mountains even the song-bird's heart
was lighter –
But in the strange land everything is strange.

I remember summer evenings, when my mother milked
the *dhrimmin,*
When the sun-rays on her white cap fell like rose-light
on the snow,
How I thought the blue eyes like to Hers, the blessed
amongst women,
And the red mouth bent and kissed me as the twilight
gathered dim in
Cool recesses where the *fraughans* hide and grow.

Then we hurry through the gloaming lest the leprechaun
belate us,
And the sheep-dog runs before us on quick-pattering,
eager feet,
For the father and the master and the supper all await us,
And no diamonds ever glistened like the froth on the
potatoes
In the three-legged skillet on the fire of peat.

Little silver flames go trembling through the blocks of
glowing amber,
Reach the unlit outer edges, strain beyond ambitiously,
Rise like baby tides of moonlight, creep and fly and spring
and clamber,
Lo! the firelight falls and flashes in the dusky, brown-
roofed chamber –
And the *gossoon* laughs upon his father's knee!

Then I hear my mother whisper, 'Let us bless Him who
    has blessed us!'
  And outside the corn-crake murmurs in the depths of
    dewy grass,
In the dim blue sky the stars come out while we lie down
    and rest us –
I've been dreaming! here I'm sitting by my fire of stiff
    asbestos,
  And my footman enters in to light the gas!

ALICE FURLONG

RINGSEND

(After reading Tolstoi)

I will live in Ringsend
With a red-headed whore,
And the fan-light gone in
Where it lights the hall-door;
And listen each night
For her querulous shout,
As at last she streels in
And the pubs empty out.
To soothe that wild breast
With my old-fangled songs,
Till she feels it redressed
From inordinate wrongs,
Imagined, outrageous,
Preposterous wrongs,
Till peace at last comes,
Shall be all I will do,
Where the little lamp blooms
Like a rose in the stew;
And up the back-garden
The sound comes to me
Of the lapsing, unsoilable,
Whispering sea.

OLIVER ST JOHN GOGARTY

GOLDEN STOCKINGS

Golden stockings you had on
In the meadow where you ran;
And your little knees together
Bobbed like pippins in the weather
When the breezes rush and fight
For those dimples of delight;
And they dance from the pursuit,
And the leaf looks like the fruit.

I have many a sight in mind
That would last if I were blind;
Many verses I could write
That would bring me many a sight.
Now I only see but one,
See you running in the sun;
And the gold-dust coming up
From the trampled butter-cup.

OLIVER ST JOHN GOGARTY

from THE DESERTED VILLAGE

Sweet smiling village, loveliest of the lawn,
Thy sports are fled, and all thy charms withdrawn;
Amidst thy bowers the tyrant's hand is seen,
And desolation saddens all thy green:
One only master grasps the whole domain,
And half a tillage stints thy smiling plain:
No more thy glassy brook reflects the day,
But chok'd with sedges, works its weedy way.
Along thy glades, a solitary guest,
The hollow-sounding bittern guards its nest;
Amidst thy desert walks the lapwing flies,
And tires their echoes with unvaried cries.
Sunk are thy bowers in shapeless ruin all,
And the long grass o'ertops the mould'ring wall;
And trembling, shrinking from the spoiler's hand,
Far, far away, thy children leave the land.

Ill fares the land, to hast'ning ills a prey,
Where wealth accumulates, and men decay:
Princes and lords may flourish, or may fade;
A breath can make them, as a breath has made;
But a bold peasantry, their country's pride,
When once destroy'd, can never be supplied.

A time there was, ere England's griefs began,
When every rood of ground maintain'd its man;
For him light labour spread her wholesome store,
Just gave what life requir'd, but gave no more:
His best companions, innocence and health;
And his best riches, ignorance of wealth.

But times are alter'd; trade's unfeeling train
Usurp the land and dispossess the swain;
Along the lawn, where scatter'd hamlets rose,

Unwieldy wealth, and cumbrous pomp repose;
And every want to opulence allied,
And every pang that folly pays to pride.

OLIVER GOLDSMITH

STANZAS: ON WOMAN

When lovely Woman stoops to folly,
    And finds too late that men betray,
What charm can soothe her melancholy,
    What art can wash her guilt away?

The only art her guilt to cover,
    To hide her shame from every eye,
To give repentance to her lover,
    And wring his bosom, is – to die.

OLIVER GOLDSMITH

MY LOVE'S AN ARBUTUS

My love's an arbutus
   By the borders of Lene,
So slender and shapely
   In her girdle of green;
And I measure the pleasure
   Of her eye's sapphire sheen
By the blue skies that sparkle
   Through that soft branching screen.

But though ruddy the berry
   And snowy the flower
That brighten together
   The arbutus bower,
Perfuming and blooming
   Through sunshine and shower,
Give *me* her bright lips
   And her laugh's pearly bower.

Alas! fruit and blossom
   Shall scatter the lea,
And Time's jealous fingers
   Dim your young charms, machree.
But unranging, unchanging,
   You'll still cling to me,
Like the evergreen leaf
   To the arbutus tree.

ALFRED PERCEVAL GRAVES

FATHER O'FLYNN

Of priests we can offer a charmin' variety,
Far renowned for larnin' and piety;
Still, I'd advance ye widout impropriety,
    Father O'Flynn as the flower of them all.

Chorus

    Here's a health to you, Father O'Flynn,
    Sláinte, and *sláinte*, and *sláinte* agin;
      Powerfulest preacher, and
      Tinderest teacher, and
    Kindliest creature in ould Donegal.

Don't talk of your Provost and Fellows of Trinity,
Famous for ever at Greek and Latinity,
Dad! and the divels and all at Divinity —
    Father O'Flynn'd make hares of them all!
      Come, I vinture to give ye my word,
      Niver the likes of his logic was heard,
        Down from mythology
        Into thayology,
    Troth! and conchology if he'd the call.

Chorus

    Here's a health to you, Father O'Flynn,
    Sláinte, and *sláinte*, and *sláinte* agin;
      Powerfulest preacher, and
      Tinderest teacher, and
    Kindliest creature in ould Donegal.

Och! Father O'Flynn, you've the wonderful way wid you,
All ould sinners are wishful to pray wid you,
All the young childer are wild for to play wid you,
    You've such a way wid you, Father avick!
      Still, for all you've so gentle a soul,
      Gad, you've your flock in the grandest control,

Checking the crazy ones,
Coaxin' onaisy ones,
Liftin' the lazy ones on wid the stick.

Chorus

Here's a health to you, Father O'Flynn,
Sláinte, and *sláinte,* and *sláinte* agin;
Powerfulest preacher, and
Tinderest teacher, and
Kindliest creature in ould Donegal.

And though quite avoidin' all foolish frivolity,
Still, at all seasons of innocent jollity,
Where was the play-boy could claim an equality
    At comicality, Father, wid you?
        Once the Bishop looked grave at your jest,
        Till this remark set him off wid the rest:
            'Is it lave gaiety
            All to the laity?
Cannot the clargy be Irishmen too?'

Chorus

Here's a health to you, Father O'Flynn,
Sláinte, and *sláinte,* and *sláinte* agin;
Powerfulest preacher, and
Tinderest teacher, and
Kindliest creature in ould Donegal.

ALFRED PERCEVAL GRAVES

EILEEN AROON

When, like the early rose,
    Eileen Aroon!
Beauty in childhood blows,
    Eileen Aroon!
When, like a diadem,
Buds blush around the stem,
Which is the fairest gem?
    Eileen Aroon!

Is it the laughing eye,
    Eileen Aroon!
Is it the timid sigh,
    Eileen Aroon!
Is it the tender tone,
Soft as the stringed harp's moan?
O it is truth alone,
    Eileen Aroon!

When, like the rising day,
    Eileen Aroon!
Love sends his early ray,
    Eileen Aroon!
What makes his dawning glow,
Changeless through joy or woe?
Only the constant know –
    Eileen Aroon!

I know a valley fair,
    Eileen Aroon!
I knew a cottage there,
    Eileen Aroon!
Far in that valley's shade
I knew a gentle maid,
Flower of a hazel glade,
    Eileen Aroon!

Who in the song so sweet?
   Eileen Aroon!
Who in the dance so fleet?
   Eileen Aroon!
Dear were her charms to me,
Dearer her laughter free,
Dearest her constancy,
   Eileen Aroon!

Were she no longer true,
   Eileen Aroon!
What should her lover do?
   Eileen Aroon!
Fly with his broken chain
Far o'er the sounding main,
Never to love again,
   Eileen Aroon!

Youth must with time decay,
   Eileen Aroon!
Beauty must fade away,
   Eileen Aroon!
Castles are sacked in war,
Chieftains are scattered far,
Truth is a fixèd star,
   Eileen Aroon!

GERALD GRIFFIN

WHO FEARS TO SPEAK OF NINETY-EIGHT?

Who fears to speak of Ninety-Eight?
Who blushes at the name?
When cowards mock the patriot's fate,
Who hangs his head for shame?
He's all a knave or half a slave
Who slights his country thus:
But a true man, like you, man,
Will fill your glass with us.

We drink the memory of the brave,
The faithful and the few –
Some lie far off beyond the wave,
Some sleep in Ireland, too;
All, all are gone – but still lives on
The fame of those who died;
And true men, like you, men,
Remember them with pride.

Some on the shores of distant lands
Their weary hearts have laid,
And by the stranger's heedless hands
Their lonely graves were made;
But though their clay be far away
Beyond the Atlantic foam,
In true men, like you, men,
Their spirit's still at home.

The dust of some is Irish earth;
Among their own they rest;
And the same land that gave them birth
Has caught them to her breast;
And we will pray that from their clay
Full many a race may start
Of true men, like you, men,
To act as brave a part.

They rose in dark and evil days
　　To right their native land;
They kindled here a living blaze
　　That nothing shall withstand.
Alas! that Might can vanquish Right —
　　They fell, and passed away;
But true men, like you, men,
　　Are plenty here today.

Then here's their memory — may it be
　　For us a guiding light,
To cheer our strife for liberty,
　　And teach us to unite!
Through good and ill, be Ireland's still,
　　Though sad as theirs, your fate;
And true men, be you, men
　　Like those of Ninety-Eight.

JOHN KELLS INGRAM

SHANCODUFF

My black hills have never seen the sun rising,
Eternally they look north towards Armagh.
Lot's wife would not be salt if she had been
Incurious as my black hills that are happy
When dawn whitens Glassdrummond chapel.

My hills hoard the bright shillings of March
While the sun searches in every pocket.
They are my Alps and I have climbed the Matterhorn
With a sheaf of hay for three perishing calves
In the field under the Big Forth of Rocksavage.

The sleety winds fondle the rushy beards of Shancoduff
While the cattle-drovers sheltering in the Featherna Bush
Look up and say: 'Who owns them hungry hills
That the water-hen and snipe must have forsaken?
A poet? Then by heavens he must be poor.'
I hear and is my heart not badly shaken?

PATRICK KAVANAGH

EPIC

I have lived in important places, times
When great events were decided, who owned
That half a rood of rock, a no-man's land
Surrounded by our pitchfork-armed claims.
I heard the Duffys shouting 'Damn your soul'
And old McCabe stripped to the waist, seen
Step the plot defying blue cast-steel –
'Here is the march along these iron-stones'.
That was the year of the Munich bother. Which
Was more important? I inclined
To lose my faith in Ballyrush and Gortin
Till Homer's ghost came whispering to my mind
He said: I made the Iliad from such
A local row. Gods make their own importance.

PATRICK KAVANAGH

A CHRISTMAS CHILDHOOD

I

One side of the potato-pits was white with frost—
How wonderful that was, how wonderful!
And when we put our ears to the paling-post
The music that came out was magical.

The light between the ricks of hay and straw
Was a hole in Heaven's gable. An apple tree
With its December-glinting fruit we saw—
O you, Eve, were the world that tempted me

To eat the knowledge that grew in clay
And death the germ within it! Now and then
I can remember something of the gay
Garden that was childhood's. Again

The tracks of cattle to a drinking-place,
A green stone lying sideways in a ditch
Or any common sight the transfigured face
Of a beauty that the world did not touch.

II

My father played the melodeon
Outside at our gate;
There were stars in the morning east
And they danced to his music.

Across the wild bogs his melodeon called
To Lennons and Callans.
As I pulled on my trousers in a hurry
I knew some strange thing had happened.

Outside in the cow-house my mother
Made the music of milking;
The light of her stable-lamp was a star
And the frost of Bethlehem made it twinkle.

A water-hen screeched in the bog,
Mass-going feet
Crunched the wafer-ice on the pot-holes,
Somebody wistfully twisted the bellows wheel.

My child poet picked out the letters
On the grey stone,
In silver the wonder of a Christmas townland,
The winking glitter of a frosty dawn.

Cassiopeia was over
Cassidy's hanging hill,
I looked and three whin bushes rode across
The horizon – the Three Wise Kings.

An old man passing said:
'Can't he make it talk' –
The melodeon. I hid in the doorway
And tightened the belt of my box-pleated coat.

I nicked six nicks on the door-post
With my penknife's big blade –
There was a little one for cutting tobacco.
And I was six Christmases of age.

My father played the melodeon,
My mother milked the cows,
And I had a prayer like a white rose pinned
On the Virgin Mary's blouse.

PATRICK KAVANAGH

MY STORY

Here's my story; the stag cries,
Winter snarls as summer dies.

The wind bullies the low sun
In poor light; the seas moan.

Shapeless bracken is turning red,
The wildgoose raises its desperate head.

Birds' wings freeze where fields are hoary.
The world is ice. That's my story.

ANONYMOUS
translated by Brendan Kennelly

KEEP YOUR KISS TO YOURSELF

Keep your kiss to yourself,
young miss with the white teeth.
I can get no taste from it.
Keep your mouth away from me.

I got a kiss more sweet than honey
from a man's wife, for love,
and I'll get no taste from any kiss
till doomsday, after that.

Until I see that same woman
(grant it, gracious Son of God)
I'll love no woman young or old
because her kiss is — what it is!

ANONYMOUS
translated by Thomas Kinsella

THE SCHOLAR'S LIFE

Sweet is the scholar's life,
busy about his studies,
the sweetest lot in Ireland
as all of you know well.

No king or prince to rule him
nor lord however mighty,
no rent to the chapterhouse,
no drudging, no dawn-rising.

Dawn-rising or shepherding
never required of him,
no need to take his turn
as watchman in the night.

He spends a while at chess,
and a while with the pleasant harp
and a further while wooing
and winning lovely women.

His horse-team hale and hearty
at the first coming of spring;
the harrow for his team
is a fistful of pens.

ANONYMOUS
translated by Thomas Kinsella

On the deck of Patrick Lynch's boat I sat in
    woeful plight,
Through my sighing all the weary day, and weeping
    all the night;
Were it not that full of sorrow from my people forth
    I go,
By the blessed sun! 'tis royally I'd sing thy
    praise, Mayo!

When I dwelt at home in plenty, and my gold did
    much abound,
In the company of fair young maids the Spanish ale
    went round —
'Tis a bitter change from those gay days that now
    I'm forced to go,
And must leave my bones in Santa Cruz, far from
    my own Mayo.

They are altered girls in Irrul now; 'tis proud they're
    grown and high,
With their hair-bags and their top-knots, for I pass
    their buckles by —
But it's little now I need their airs, for God will
    have it so,
That I must depart for foreign lands, and leave my
    sweet Mayo.

'Tis my grief that Patrick Loughlin is not Earl of Irrul still,
And that Brian Duff no longer rules as Lord upon
    the hill:
And that Colonel Hugh MacGrady should be lying
    dead and low,

And I sailing, sailing swiftly from the county
of Mayo.

THOMAS LAVELLE
translated by George Fox

THE HERONS

As I was climbing Ardan Mór
From the shore of Sheelin lake,
I met the herons coming down
Before the water's wake.

And they were talking in their flight
Of dreamy ways the herons go
When all the hills were withered up
Nor any waters flow.

FRANCIS LEDWIDGE

THOMAS MacDONAGH

He shall not hear the bittern cry
In the wild sky, where he is lain,
Nor voices of the sweeter birds
Above the wailing of the rain.

Nor shall he know when loud March blows
Thro' slanting snows her fanfare shrill,
Blowing to flame the golden cup
Of many an upset daffodil.

But when the Dark Cow leaves the moor,
And pastures poor with greedy weeds,
Perhaps he'll hear her low at morn
Lifting her horn in pleasant meads.

FRANCIS LEDWIDGE

THE WIDOW OF DRYNAM

I stand in my door and look over the low fields of Drynam.
No man but the one man has known me, no child but the one
Grew big at my breast, and what are my sorrows beside
That pride and that glory? I come from devotions on Sunday
And leave them to pity or spite; and though I who had music
    have none
But crying of seagulls at morning and calling of curlews at
    night,
I wake and remember my beauty and think of my son
Who would stare the loud fools into silence
And rip the dull parish asunder.

Small wonder indeed he was wild with breeding and beauty
And why would my proud lad not straighten his back from
    the plough?
My son was not got and I bound in a cold bed of duty
Nor led to the side of the road by some clay-clabbered lout!
No, but rapt by a passionate poet away from the dancers
To curtains and silver and firelight –
O wisely and gently he drew down the pale shell of satin
And all the bright evening's adornment and clad me
Again in the garment of glory, the joy of his eyes.

I stand in my door and look over the low fields of Drynam
When skies move westward, the way he will come from the
    war;
Maybe on a morning of March when a thin sun is shining
And starlings have blackened the thorn,
He will come, my bright limb of glory, my mettlesome wild
    one,
With coin in his pocket and tales on the tip of his tongue,

And the proud ones that slight me will bring back forgotten
    politeness
To see me abroad on the roads with my son,
The two of us laughing together or stepping in silence.

PATRICK MACDONOGH

JOHN-JOHN

I dreamt last night of you, John-John,
  And thought you called to me;
And when I woke this morning, John,
  Yourself I hoped to see;
But I was all alone, John-John,
  Though still I heard your call;
I put my boots and bonnet on,
  And took my Sunday shawl,
And went, full sure to find you, John,
  At Nenagh fair.

The fair was just the same as then,
  Five years ago to-day,
When first you left the thimble men
  And came with me away;
For there again were thimble men
  And shooting galleries,
And card-trick men and Maggie-men,
  Of all sorts and degrees;
But not a sight of you, John-John,
  Was anywhere.

I turned my face to home again,
  And called myself a fool
To think you'd leave the thimble men
  And live again by rule,
And go to mass and keep the fast
  And till the little patch:
My wish to have you home was past
  Before I raised the latch
And pushed the door and saw you, John,
  Sitting down there.

How cool you came in here, begad,
　　As if you owned the place!
But rest yourself there now, my lad,
　　'Tis good to see your face;
My dream is out, and now by it
　　I think I know my mind:
At six o'clock this house you'll quit,
　　And leave no grief behind; –
But until six o'clock, John-John,
　　My bit you'll share.

The neighbours' shame of me began
　　When first I brought you in;
To wed and keep a tinker man
　　They thought a kind of sin;
But now this three year since you're gone
　　'Tis pity me they do,
And that I'd rather have, John-John,
　　Than that they'd pity you,
Pity for me and you, John-John,
　　I could not bear.

Oh, you're my husband right enough,
　　But what's the good of that?
You know you never were the stuff
　　To be the cottage cat,
To watch the fire and hear me lock
　　The door and put out Shep –
But there, now, it is six o'clock
　　And time for you to step.
God bless and keep you far, John-John!
　　And that's my prayer.

THOMAS MACDONAGH

THE CELTS

Long, long ago, beyond the misty space
    Of twice a thousand years,
In Erin old there dwelt a mighty race,
    Taller than Roman spears;
Like oaks and towers they had a giant grace,
    Were fleet as deers,
With wind and waves they made their 'biding place,
    These western shepherd seers.

Their Ocean-God was Manannan MacLir,
    Whose angry lips,
In their white foam, full often would inter
    Whole fleets of ships;
Cromah their Day-God, and their Thunderer
    Made morning and eclipse;
Bride was their Queen of Song, and unto her
    They prayed with fire-touched lips.

Great were their deeds, their passions and their sports;
    With clay and stone
They piled on strath and shore those mystic forts,
    Not yet o'erthrown;
On cairn-crowned hills they held their council-courts;
    While youths alone,
With giant dogs, explored the elk resorts,
    And brought them down.

Of these was Finn, the father of the Bard,
    Whose ancient song
Over the clamour of all change is heard,
    Sweet-voiced and strong.
Finn once o'ertook Grania, the golden-haired,
    The fleet and young;
From her the lovely, and from him the feared,
    The primal poet sprung.

Ossian! two thousand years of mist and change
    Surround thy name –
Thy Fenian heroes now no longer range
    The hills of fame.
Thy very names of Finn and Gaul sound strange –
    Yet thine the same –
By miscalled lake and desecrated grange –
    Remains, and shall remain!

The Druid's altar and the Druid's creed
    We scarce can trace,
There is not left an undisputed deed
    Of all your race,
Save your majestic song, which hath their speed,
    And strength and grace;
In that sole song, they live and love, and bleed –
    It bears them on through space.

O, inspired giant! shall we e'er behold,
    In our own time,
One fit to speak your spirit on the wold,
    Or seize your rhyme?
One pupil of the past, as mighty-souled
    As in the prime,
Were the fond, fair, and beautiful, and bold –
    They of your song sublime!

THOMAS D'ARCY McGEE

THE YELLOW BITTERN

The yellow bittern that never broke out
    In a drinking bout, might as well have drunk;
His bones are thrown on a naked stone
    Where he lived alone like a hermit monk.
O yellow bittern! I pity your lot,
    Though they say that a sot like myself is curst—
I was sober a while, but I'll drink and be wise
    For I fear I should die in the end of thirst.

It's not for the common birds that I'd mourn,
    The black-bird, the corn-crake, or the crane,
But for the bittern that's shy and apart
    And drinks in the marsh from the lone bog-drain.
Oh! if I had known you were near your death,
    While my breath held out I'd have run to you,
Till a splash from the Lake of the Son of the Bird
    Your soul would have stirred and waked anew.

My darling told me to drink no more
    Or my life would be o'er in a little short while;
But I told her 'tis drink gives me health and strength
    And will lengthen my road by many a mile.
You see how the bird of the long smooth neck
    Could get his death from the thirst at last—
Come, son of my soul, and drain your cup,
    You'll get no sup when your life is past.

In a wintering island by Constantine's halls
    A bittern calls from a wineless place,
And tells me that hither he cannot come
    Till the summer is here and the sunny days.
When he crosses the stream there and wings o'er the sea
    Then a fear comes to me he may fail in his flight—

Well, the milk and the ale are drunk every drop,
And a dram won't stop our thirst this night.

CATHAL BUÍ MACGIOLLA GHUNNA
translated by Thomas MacDonagh

KINCORA

O, where, Kincora! is Brian the Great?
 And where is the beauty that once was thine?
O, where are the princes and nobles that sate
 At the feast in thy halls, and drank the red wine?
         Where, O Kincora?

O, where, Kincora! are thy valorous lords?
 O, whither, thou Hospitable! are they gone?
O, where are the Dalcassians of the Golden Swords?
 And where are the warriors Brian led on?
         Where, O Kincora?

And where is Murrough, the descendant of kings –
 The defeater of a hundred – the daringly brave –
Who set but slight store by jewels and rings –
 Who swam down the torrent and laughed at its wave?
         Where, O Kincora?

And where is Donogh, King Brian's worthy son?
 And where is Conaing, the Beautiful Chief?
And Kian and Corc? Alas! they are gone –
 They have left me this night alone with my grief.
         Left me, Kincora!

And where are the chiefs with whom Brian went forth,
 The never-vanquished sons of Erin the brave,
The great King of Onaght, renowned for his worth,
 And the hosts of Baskinn from the western wave?
         Where, O Kincora?

O, where is Duvlann of the swift-footed Steeds?
 And where is Kian, who was son of Molloy?
And where is King Lonergan, the fame of whose deeds
 In the red battle-field no time can destroy?
         Where, O Kincora?

And where is that youth of majestic height,
    The faith-keeping Prince of the Scots? Even he,
As wide as his fame was, as great as was his might,
    Was tributary, O Kincora, to thee!
                                        Thee, O Kincora!

They are gone, those heroes of royal birth,
    Who plundered no churches, and broke no trust,
'Tis weary for me to be living on earth
    When they, O Kincora, lie low in the dust!
                                        Low, O Kincora!

O, never again will Princes appear,
    To rival the Dalcassians of the Cleaving Swords!
I can never dream of meeting afar or anear,
    In the east or the west, such heroes and lords!
                                        Never, Kincora!

O, dear are the images my memory calls up
    Of Brian Boru! – how he never would miss
To give me at the banquet the first bright cup!
    Ah! why did he heap on me honour like this?
                                        Why, O Kincora?

I am Mac Liag, and my home is on the Lake:
    Thither often, to that palace whose beauty is fled
Came Brian to ask me, and I went for his sake.
    O, my grief! that I should live, and Brian be dead!
                                        Dead, O Kincora!

MAC LIAG
translated by James Clarence Mangan

MEETING POINT

Time was away and somewhere else,
There were two glasses and two chairs
And two people with the one pulse
(Somebody stopped the moving stairs):
Time was away and somewhere else.

And they were neither up nor down;
The stream's music did not stop
Flowing through heather, limpid brown,
Although they sat in a coffee shop
And they were neither up nor down.

The bell was silent in the air
Holding its inverted poise –
Between the clang and clang a flower,
A brazen calyx of no noise:
The bell was silent in the air.

The camels crossed the miles of sand
That stretched around the cups and plates;
The desert was their own, they planned
To portion out the stars and dates:
The camels crossed the miles of sand.

Time was away and somewhere else.
The waiter did not come, the clock
Forgot them and the radio waltz
Came out like water from a rock:
Time was away and somewhere else.

Her fingers flicked away the ash
That bloomed again in tropic trees:
Not caring if the markets crash
When they had forests such as these,
Her fingers flicked away the ash.

God or whatever means the Good
Be praised that time can stop like this,
That what the heart has understood
Can verify in the body's peace
God or whatever means the Good.

Time was away and she was here
And life no longer what it was,
The bell was silent in the air
And all the room one glow because
Time was away and she was here.

LOUIS MACNEICE

DARK ROSALEEN

O my Dark Rosaleen,
   Do not sigh, do not weep!
The priests are on the ocean green,
   They march along the Deep.
There's wine. . . from the royal Pope
   Upon the ocean green;
And Spanish ale shall give you hope,
   My Dark Rosaleen!
   My own Rosaleen!
Shall glad your heart, shall give you hope,
Shall give you health, and help, and hope,
   My Dark Rosaleen.

Over hills and through dales,
   Have I roamed for your sake;
All yesterday I sailed with sails
   On river and on lake.
The Erne. . . at its highest flood
   I dashed across unseen,
For there was lightning in my blood,
   My Dark Rosaleen!
   My own Rosaleen!
Oh! there was lightning in my blood,
Red lightning lightened through my blood,
   My Dark Rosaleen!

All day long in unrest
   To and fro do I move,
The very soul within my breast
   Is wasted for you, love!
The heart. . . in my bosom faints
   To think of you, my Queen,
My life of life, my saint of saints,
   My Dark Rosaleen!
   My own Rosaleen!

To hear your sweet and sad complaints,
My life, my love, my saint of saints,
   My Dark Rosaleen!

Woe and pain, pain and woe,
   Are my lot night and noon,
To see your bright face clouded so,
   Like to the mournful moon.
But yet. . . will I rear your throne
   Again in golden sheen;
'Tis you shall reign, shall reign alone,
   My Dark Rosaleen!
   My own Rosaleen!
'Tis you shall have the golden throne,
'Tis you shall reign, and reign alone,
   My Dark Rosaleen!

Over dews, over sands
   Will I fly for your weal;
Your holy delicate white hands
   Shall girdle me with steel.
At home. . . in your emerald bowers,
   From morning's dawn till e'en,
You'll pray for me, my flower of flowers,
   My Dark Rosaleen!
   My fond Rosaleen!
You'll think of me through daylight's hours,
My virgin flower, my flower of flowers,
   My Dark Rosaleen!

I could scale the blue air,
   I could plough the high hills,
Oh, I could kneel all night in prayer,
   To heal your many ills!
And one. . . beamy smile from you

Would float like light between
My toils and me, my own, my true,
  My Dark Rosaleen!
  My fond Rosaleen!
Would give me life and soul anew,
A second life, a soul anew,
  My Dark Rosaleen!

O! the Erne shall run red
  With redundance of blood,
The earth shall rock beneath our tread,
  And flames wrap hill and wood,
And gun-peal, and slogan cry,
  Wake many a glen serene,
Ere you shall fade, ere you shall die,
  My Dark Rosaleen!
  My own Rosaleen!
The Judgement Hour must first be nigh,
Ere you can fade, ere you can die,
  My Dark Rosaleen!

OWEN ROE MAC WARD
translated by James Clarence Mangan

THE WOMAN OF THREE COWS

O Woman of Three Cows, *agra*! don't let your tongue thus rattle!
O, don't be saucy, don't be stiff, because you may have cattle.
I have seen – and, here's my hand to you, I only say what's true –
A many a one with twice your stock not half so proud as you.

Good luck to you, don't scorn the poor, and don't be their
    despiser,
For worldly wealth soon melts away, and cheats the very miser,
And Death soon strips the proudest wreath from haughty human
    brows;
Then don't be stiff, and don't be proud, good Woman of Three
    Cows!

See where Momonia's heroes lie, proud Owen More's
    descendants,
'Tis they that won the glorious name, and had the grand
    attendants!
If *they* were forced to bow to Fate, as every mortal bows,
Can *you* be proud, can *you* be stiff, my Woman of Three Cows!

The brave sons of the Lord of Clare, they left the land to
    mourning;
Mavrone! for they were banished, with no hope of their
    returning –
Who knows in what abodes of want those youths were driven to
    house?
Yet *you* can give yourself these airs, O Woman of Three Cows!

O, think of Donnell of the Ships, the Chief whom nothing
    daunted –
See how he fell in distant Spain, unchronicled, unchanted!
He sleeps, the great O'Sullivan, where thunder cannot rouse –
Then ask yourself, should *you* be proud, good Woman of Three
    Cows!

O'Ruark, Maguire, those souls of fire, whose names are shrined in
    story —
Think how their high achievements once made Erin's highest
    glory —
Yet now their bones lie mouldering under weeds and cypress
    boughs,
And so, for all your pride, will yours, O Woman of Three Cows!

The O'Carrolls, also, famed when Fame was only for the boldest,
Rest in forgotten sepulchres with Erin's best and oldest;
Yet who so great as they of yore in battle or carouse?
Just think of that, and hide your head, good Woman of Three
    Cows!

Your neighbour's poor, and you, it seems, are big with vain ideas,
Because, *inagh*! you've got three cows — one more, I see, than
    she has.
That tongue of yours wags more at times than Charity allows,
But if you're strong, be merciful, great Woman of Three Cows!

The Summing Up

Now, there you go! You still, of course, keep up your scornful
    bearing,
And I'm too poor to hinder you; but, by the cloak I'm wearing,
If I had but *four* cows myself, even though you were my spouse,
I'd thwack you well to cure your pride, my Woman of Three
    Cows!

ANONYMOUS
translated by James Clarence Mangan

from THE MIDNIGHT COURT

I

I liked to walk in the river meadows
In the thick of the dew and the morning shadows,
At the edge of the woods in a deep defile
At peace with myself in the first sunshine.
When I looked at Lough Graney my heart grew bright,
Ploughed lands and green in the morning light,
Mountains in rows with crimson borders
Peering above their neighbours' shoulders.
The heart that never had known relief
In a lonesome old man distraught with grief,
Without money or home or friends or ease,
Would quicken to glimpse beyond the trees
The ducks sail by on a mistless bay
And a swan before them lead the way;
A speckled trout that in their track
Splashed in the air with arching back;
The grey of the lake and the waves around
That foamed at its edge with a hollow sound.
Birds in the trees sang merry and loud;
A fawn flashed out of the shadowy wood;
The horns rang out with the huntsman's cry
And the belling of hounds while the fox slipped by.

Yesterday morning the sky was clear,
The sun fell hot on river and mere,
Its horses fresh and with gamesome eye
Harnessed again to assail the sky;
The leaves were thick upon every bough
And ferns and grass were thick below,
Sheltering bowers of herbs and flowers
That would comfort a man in his dreariest hours.
Longing for sleep bore down my head,
And in the grass I scooped a bed

With a hollow behind to house my back,
A prop for my head and my limbs stretched slack.
What more could one ask? I covered my face
To avert the flies as I dozed a space,
But my mind in dreams was filled with grief
And I tossed and groaned as I sought relief.

I had only begun when I felt a shock,
And all the landscape seemed to rock;
A north wind made my senses tingle
And thunder crackled along the shingle.
As I looked up — as I thought, awake —
I seemed to see at the edge of the lake
As ugly a brute as man could see
In the shape of woman approaching me;
For, if I calculated right,
She must have been twenty feet in height,
With yards and yards of hairy cloak
Trailing behind her in the muck.
There never was seen such a freak of nature;
Without a single presentable feature;
Her grinning jaws with the fangs stuck out
Would be cause sufficient to start a rout,
And in a hand like a weaver's beam
She raised a staff that it might be seen
She was coming on a legal errand,
For nailed to the staff was a bailiff's warrant.

She cried in a voice with a brassy ring:
'Get up out of that, you lazy thing!
That a man like you could think 'tis fitting
To lie in a ditch while the court is sitting!
A decenter court than e'er you knew,
And far too good for the likes of you.
Justice and Mercy hand in hand

Sit in the courts of Fairyland.
Let Ireland think when her trouble's ended
Of those by whom she was befriended.
In Moy Graney palace twelve days and nights
They've sat discussing your wrongs and rights.
All mourned that follow in his train,
Like the king himself, that in his reign
Such unimaginable disaster
Should follow your people, man and master.
Old stock uprooted on every hand
Without claim to rent or law or land;
Nothing to see in a land defiled
Where the flowers were plucked but the weeds ran wild;
The best of your breed in foreign places,
And upstart rogues with impudent faces,
Planning with all their guile and spleen
To pick the bones of the Irish clean.
But worst of all those bad reports
Was that truth was darkened in their courts,
And nothing to back a poor man's case
But whispers, intrigue and the lust for place;
The lawyer's craft and the rich man's might,
Cozening, favour, greed and spite;
Maddened with jobs and bribes and malice,
Anarchy loose on cot and palace.

''Twas all discussed, and along with the rest
There were women in scores who came to attest —
A plea that concerns yourself as well —
That the youth of the country's gone to hell,
And men's increase is a sort of crime,
Which only happened within our time;
Nothing but weeds for want of tillage
Since famine and war assailed the village,
And a flighty king and emigration —

And what have you done to restore the nation?
Shame on you without chick nor child
With women in thousands running wild!
The blossoming tree and the young green shoot,
The strap that would sleep with any old root,
The little white saint at the altar rail,
And the proud, cold girl like a ship in sail –
What matter to you if their beauty founder,
If belly and breast will never be rounder,
If, ready and glad to be mother and wife,
They drop unplucked from the boughs of life?

And having considered all reports,
They agreed that in place of the English courts,
They should select a judge by lot
Who'd hold enquiry on the spot.
Then Eevul, Queen of the Grey Rock,
Who rules all Munster herd and flock,
Arose, and offered to do her share
By putting an end to injustice there.
She took an oath to the council then
To judge the women and the men,
Stand by the poor though all ignore them
And humble the pride of the rich before them;
Make might without right conceal its face
And use her might to give right its place.
Her favour money will not buy,
No lawyer will pull the truth awry,
The smoothest perjurer will not dare
To make a show of falsehood there.
The court is sitting today in Feakle,
So off with you now as quick as you're able!
Come on, I say, and give no back chat,
Or I'll take my stick and knock you flat.'
With the crook of her staff she hooked my cape,

And we went at a speed to make Christians gape
Away through the glens in one wild rush
Till we stood in Moinmoy by the ruined church.

BRYAN MERRYMAN
translated by Frank O'Connor

This hymn is also known as 'Patrick's Breastplate'.

I arise today
Through a mighty strength, the invocation of the Trinity,
Through belief in the threeness,
Through confession of the oneness
Of the Creator of Creation.

I arise today
Through the strength of Christ's birth with His baptism,
Through the strength of His crucifixion with His burial,
Through the strength of His resurrection with His ascension,
Through the strength of His descent for the judgement of
    Doom.

I arise today
Through the strength of the love of Cherubim,
In obedience of angels,
In the service of archangels,
In hope of resurrection to meet with reward,
In prayers of patriarchs,
In predictions of prophets,
In preaching of apostles,
In faiths of confessors,
In innocence of holy virgins,
In deeds of righteous men.

I arise today
Through the strength of heaven:
Light of sun,
Radiance of moon,
Splendour of fire,
Speed of lightning,
Swiftness of wind,
Depth of sea,

Stability of earth,
Firmness of rock.

I arise today
Through God's strength to pilot me:
God's might to uphold me,
God's wisdom to guide me,
God's eye to look before me,
God's ear to hear me,
God's word to speak for me,
God's hand to guard me,
God's way to lie before me,
God's shield to protect me,
God's host to save me
From snares of devils,
From temptations of vices,
From every one who shall wish me ill,
Afar and anear,
Alone and in a multitude.

I summon today all these powers between me and those evils,
Against every cruel merciless power that may oppose my body
    and soul,
Against incantations of false prophets,
Against black laws of pagandom,
Against false laws of heretics,
Against craft of idolatry,
Against spells of women and smiths and wizards,
Against every knowledge that corrupts man's body and soul.

Christ to shield me today
Against poison, against burning,
Against drowning, against wounding,
So that there may come to me abundance of reward.
Christ with me, Christ before me, Christ behind me,

Christ in me, Christ beneath me, Christ above me,
Christ on my right, Christ on my left,
Christ when I lie down, Christ when I sit down, Christ when
    I arise,
Christ in the heart of every man who thinks of me,
Christ in the mouth of every one who speaks of me,
Christ in every eye that sees me,
Christ in every ear that hears me.

I arise today
Through a mighty strength, the invocation of the Trinity,
Through belief in the threeness,
Through confession of the oneness
Of the Creator of Creation.

ANONYMOUS
translated by Kuno Meyer

THE OLD WOMAN OF BEARE

Ebb tide to me as of the sea!
Old age causes me reproach.
Though I may grieve thereat —
Happiness comes out of fat.

I am the Old Woman of Beare,
An ever-new smock I used to wear:
Today — such is my mean estate —
I wear not even a cast-off shift.

It is riches
Ye love, it is not men:
In the time when *we* lived
It was men.

Swift chariots,
And steeds that carried off the prize —
Their day of plenty has been,
A blessing on the King who lent them!

My body with bitterness has dropt
Towards the abode we know:
When the Son of God deems it time
Let Him come to deliver His behest.

My arms when they are seen
Now are bony and thin:
Once they would fondle and caress
The bodies of glorious kings.

When my arms are seen,
And they bony and thin,
They are not fit, I declare,
To be raised over comely men.

The maidens rejoice
When May-day comes to them:
For me, sorrow the share;
I am wretched, I am an old hag.

I hold no sweet converse.
No wethers are killed for my wedding-feast,
My hair is all but grey,
The mean veil over it is no pity.

I do not deem it ill
That a white veil be on my head;
Time was when cloths of every hue
Bedecked my head as we drank good ale.

The Stone of the Kings on Femen,
The Chair of Ronan in Bregon,
Long since storms have reached them:
The slabs of their tombs are old and decayed.

The wave of the great sea talks aloud,
Winter has arisen:
Fermuid the son of Mugh to-day
I do not expect on a visit.

I know what they are doing:
They row and row across
The reeds of the Ford of Alma –
Cold is the place where they sleep.

’Tis ‘O my God!’
To me today, whatever will come of it.
I must cover myself even in the sun:
The time is at hand that shall renew me.

Youth's summer in which we were
I have spent with its autumn:
Winter-age which overwhelms all men,
To me has come its beginning.

Amen! Woe is me!
Every acorn has to drop
After feasting by shining candles
To be in the gloom of a prayer-house!

I had my day with kings
Drinking mead and wine:
To-day I drink whey-water
Among shrivelled old hags.

I see upon my cloak the hair of old age,
My reason has beguiled me:
Grey is the hair that grows through my skin—
'Tis thus! I am an old woman.

The flood-wave
And the second ebb tide—
They have reached me,
I know them well.

The flood wave
Will not reach the silence of my kitchen:
Though many are my company in darkness,
A hand has been laid upon them all.

O happy the isle of the great sea
Which the flood reaches after the ebb!
As for me, I do not expect
Flood after ebb to come to me.

There is scarce a little place to-day
That I can recognise:
What was on flood
Is all on ebb.

ANONYMOUS
translated by Kuno Meyer

THE SON OF THE KING OF THE MOY

The son of the King of the Moy
met a girl in green woods on midsummer's day:
she gave him black fruit from thorns
and the full of his arms
of strawberries, where they lay.

ANONYMOUS
translated by John Montague

THE VIKINGS

Bitter the wind tonight,
combing the sea's hair white:
from the North, no need to fear
the proud sea-coursing warrior.

ANONYMOUS
translated by John Montague

BELFAST LOUGH

The whistle
of the bright
yellow billed
    little bird:

Over the loch
upon a golden
whin, a blackbird
    stirred.

ANONYMOUS
translated by John Montague

THE LIGHT OF OTHER DAYS

Oft, in the stilly night,
Ere Slumber's chain hath bound me,
Fond Memory brings the light
Of other days around me:
The smiles, the tears,
Of boyhood's years,
The words of love then spoken:
The eyes that shone,
Now dimm'd and gone,
The cheerful hearts now broken!
Thus, in the stilly night,
Ere Slumber's chain hath bound me,
Sad Memory brings the light
Of other days around me.

When I remember all
The friends, so link'd together,
I've seen around me fall,
Like leaves in wintry weather,
I feel like one
Who treads alone
Some banquet-hall deserted,
Whose lights are fled,
Whose garlands dead,
And all but he departed!
Thus, in the stilly night,
Ere Slumber's chain hath bound me,
Sad Memory brings the light
Of other days around me.

THOMAS MOORE

THE HARP THAT ONCE THROUGH TARA'S HALLS

The harp that once through Tara's halls
The soul of music shed,
Now hangs as mute on Tara's walls
As if that soul were fled.
So sleeps the pride of former days,
So glory's thrill is o'er,
And hearts, that once beat high for praise,
Now feel that pulse no more.

No more to chiefs and ladies bright
The harp of Tara swells;
The chord alone, that breaks at night,
Its tale of ruin tells.
Thus freedom now so seldom wakes,
The only throb she gives,
Is when some heart indignant breaks,
To show that still she lives.

THOMAS MOORE

THE MEETING OF THE WATERS

There is not in the wide world a valley so sweet
As that vale in whose bosom the bright waters meet;
Oh! the last rays of feeling and life must depart,
Ere the bloom of that valley shall fade from my heart.

Yet it *was* not that Nature had shed o'er the scene
Her purest of crystal and brightest of green;
'Twas *not* her soft magic of streamlet or hill,
Oh! no – it was something more exquisite still.

'Twas that friends, the belov'd of my bosom, were near,
Who made every dear scene of enchantment more dear,
And who felt how the best charms of nature improve,
When we see them reflected from looks that we love.

Sweet vale of Avoca! how calm could I rest
In thy bosom of shade, with the friends I love best,
Where the storms that we feel in this cold world should cease,
And our hearts, like thy waters, be mingled in peace.

THOMAS MOORE

THE HERMIT'S SONG

A hiding tuft, a green-barked yew-tree
   Is my roof,
While nearby a great oak keeps me
   Tempest-proof.

I can pick my fruit from an apple
   Like an inn,
Or can fill my fist where hazels
   Shut me in.

A clear well beside me offers
   Best of drink,
And there grows a bed of cresses
   Near its brink.

Pigs and goats, the friendliest neighbours,
   Nestle near,
Wild swine come, or broods of badgers,
   Grazing deer.

All the gentry of the county
   Come to call
And the foxes come behind them,
   Best of all.

To what meals the woods invite me
   All about!
There are water, herbs and cresses,
   Salmon, trout.

A clutch of eggs, sweet mast and honey
   Are my meat,
Heathberries and whortleberries
   For a sweet.

All that one could ask for comfort
   Round me grows,
There are hips and haws and strawberries,
   Nuts and sloes.

And when summer spreads its mantle
   What a sight!
Marjoram and leeks and pignuts,
   Juicy, bright.

Dainty redbreasts briskly forage
   Every bush,
Round and round my hut there flutter
   Swallow, thrush.

Bees and beetles, music-makers,
   Croon and strum;
Geese pass over, duck in autumn,
   Dark streams hum.

Angry wren, officious linnet
   And black-cap,
All industrious, and the woodpecker's
   Sturdy tap.

From the sea the gulls and herons
   Flutter in,
While in upland heather rises
   The grey hen.

In the year's most brilliant weather
   Heifers low
Through green fields, not driven nor beaten,
   Tranquil, slow.

In wreathed boughs the wind is whispering,
   Skies are blue,
Swans call, river water falling
   Is calling too.

ANONYMOUS
translated by Frank O'Connor

KILCASH

What shall we do for timber?
   The last of the woods is down.
Kilcash and the house of its glory
   And the bell of the house are gone,
The spot where that lady waited
   Who shamed all women for grace
When earls came sailing to greet her
   And Mass was said in the place.

My grief and my affliction
   Your gates are taken away,
Your avenue needs attention,
   Goats in the garden stray.
The courtyard's filled with water
   And the great earls where are they?
The earls, the lady, the people
   Beaten into the clay.

No sound of duck or geese there,
   Hawk's cry or eagle's call,
No humming of the bees there
   That brought honey and wax for all,
Nor even the song of the birds there

When the sun goes down in the west,
No cuckoo on top of the boughs there,
   Singing the world to rest.

There's mist there tumbling from branches,
   Unstirred by night and by day,
And darkness falling from heaven,
   For our fortune has ebbed away,
There's no holly nor hazel nor ash there,
   The pasture's rock and stone,
The crown of the forest has withered,
   And the last of its game is gone.

I beseech of Mary and Jesus
   That the great come home again
With long dances danced in the garden,
   Fiddle music and mirth among men,
That Kilcash the home of our fathers
   Be lifted on high again,
And from that to the deluge of waters
   In bounty and peace remain.

ANONYMOUS
translated by Frank O'Connor

ON THE DEATH OF HIS WIFE

I parted from my life last night,
  A woman's body sunk in clay:
The tender bosom that I loved
  Wrapped in a sheet they took away.

The heavy blossom that had lit
  The ancient boughs is tossed and blown;
Hers was the burden of delight
  That long had weighed the old tree down.

And I am left alone tonight
  And desolate is the world I see
For lovely was that woman's weight
  That even last night had lain on me.

Weeping I look upon the place
  Where she used to rest her head –
For yesterday her body's length
  Reposed upon you too, my bed.

Yesterday that smiling face
  Upon one side of you was laid
That could match the hazel bloom
  In its dark delicate sweet shade.

Maelva of the shadowy brows
  Was the mead-cask at my side;
Fairest of all flowers that grow
  Was the beauty that has died.

My body's self deserts me now,
  The half of me that was her own,
Since all I knew of brightness died
  Half of me lingers, half is gone.

The face that was like hawthorn bloom
   Was my right foot and my right side;
And my right hand and my right eye
   Were no more mine than hers who died.

Poor is the share of me that's left
   Since half of me died with my wife;
I shudder at the words I speak;
   Dear God, that girl was half my life.

And our first look was her first love;
   No man had fondled ere I came
The little breasts so small and firm
   And the long body like a flame.

For twenty years we shared a home,
   Our converse milder with each year;
Eleven children in its time
   Did that tall stately body bear.

It was the King of hosts and roads
   Who snatched her from me in her prime:
Little she wished to leave alone
   The man she loved before her time.

Now King of churches and of bells,
   Though never raised to pledge a lie
That woman's hand – can it be true? –
   No more beneath my head will lie.

MUIREADACH Ó DALAIGH
translated by Frank O'Connor

from THE LAMENT FOR ART O'LEARY

My love and my delight,
The day I saw you first
Beside the market-house
  I had eyes for nothing else
  And love for none but you.

  I left my father's house
  And ran away with you,
  And that was no bad choice;
  You gave me everything.
There were parlours whitened for me,
Bedrooms painted for me,
Ovens reddened for me,
Loaves baked for me,
Joints spitted for me,
Beds made for me
To take my ease on flock
Until the milking time
And later if I pleased.

My mind remembers
That bright spring day,
How your hat with its band
Of gold became you,
Your silver-hilted sword,
Your manly right hand,
Your horse on her mettle
And foes around you
Cowed by your air;
For when you rode by
On your white-nosed mare
The English lowered their head before you
Not out of love for you
But hate and fear,

For, sweetheart of my soul,
The English killed you.

My love and my calf
Of the race of the Earls of Antrim
And the Barrys of Eemokilly,
How well a sword became you,
A hat with a band,
A slender foreign shoe
And a suit of yarn
Woven over the water!

My love and my darling
When I go home
The little lad, Conor,
And Fiach the baby
Will surely ask me
Where I left their father,
I'll say with anguish
'Twas in Kilnamartyr;
They will call the father
Who will never answer.

My love and my mate
That I never thought dead
Till your horse came to me
With bridle trailing,
All blood from forehead
To polished saddle
Where you should be,
Either sitting or standing;
I gave one leap to the threshold,
A second to the gate,
A third upon its back.

I clapped my hands,
And off at a gallop;
I never lingered
Till I found you lying
By a little furze-bush
Without pope or bishop
Or priest or cleric
One prayer to whisper
But an old, old woman,
And her cloak about you,
And your blood in torrents –
Art O'Leary –
I did not wipe it off,
I drank it from my palms.

My love and my delight
Stand up now beside me,
And let me lead you home
Until I make a feast,
And I will roast the meat
And send for company
And call the harpers in,
And I shall make your bed
Of soft and snowy sheets
And blankets dark and rough
To warm the beloved limbs
An autumn blast has chilled.

EILEEN O'LEARY
translated by Frank O'Connor

CORRYMEELA

Over here in England I'm helpin' wi' the hay,
And I wisht I was in Ireland the livelong day;
Weary on the English hay, an' sorra take the
    wheat!
Och! Corrymeela, an' the blue sky over it.

There's a deep dumb river flowin' by beyont the
    heavy trees,
This livin' air is moithered wi' the hummin' o' the
    bees;
I wisht I'd hear the Claddagh burn go runnin'
    through the heat
Past Corrymeela, wi' the blue sky over it.

The people that's in England is richer nor the
    Jews,
There's not the smallest young gossoon but
    thravels in his shoes!
I'd give the pipe between me teeth to see a barefut
    child,
Och! Corrymeela, an' the low south wind.

Here's hands so full o' money an' hearts so full
    o' care,
By the luck o' love! I'd still go light for all I did
    go bare.
'God save ye, *colleen dhas,*' I said; the girl she
    thought me wild!
Far Corrymeela, an' the low south wind.

D'ye mind me now, the song at night is mortial
    hard to raise,
The girls are heavy-goin' here, the boys are ill to
    plase;

When ones't I'm out this workin' hive, 'tis I'll
     be back again –
Aye, Corrymeela, in the same soft rain.

The puff o' smoke from one ould roof before an
     English town!
For a *shaugh* wid Andy Feelan here I'd give a
     silver crown,
For a curl o' hair like Mollie's ye'll ask the like in
     vain,
Sweet Corrymeela, an' the same soft rain.

MOIRA O'NEILL

VALENTINE BROWNE

A mist of pain has covered my dour old heart
since the alien devils entered the land of Conn;
our Western Sun, Munster's right ruler, clouded
— there's the reason I'd ever to call on you, Valentine Browne.

First, Cashel's company gone, its guest-houses and youth;
the gabled palace of Brian flooded dark with otters;
Ealla left leaderless, lacking royal Munster sons
— there's the reason I'd ever to call on you, Valentine Browne.

The deer has altered her erstwhile noble shape
since the alien raven roosted in Ros's fastness;
fish fled the sunlit stream and the quiet current
— there's the reason I'd ever to call on you, Valentine Browne.

Dairinis in the West with no Earl of the noble race;
in Hamburg, to our cost, that Earl over gay peaceful hawks;
and these old grey eyes weeping for both these things
— there's the reason I'd ever to call on you, Valentine Browne.

Feathers of the swift bird-flock drift on the wind
tattered like a cat's fur in a waste of heather;
cattle deny the flow of milk to their calves
— since 'Sir Val' walked into the rights of the gentle Carthy.

Into the uplands Pan directed his gaze
to see where that Mars vanished, who left us to die.
Dwarf monsters have taken up the Blade of the Three
and hacked our dead across from heel to top.

AOGÁN Ó RATHAILLE
translated by Thomas Kinsella

from ODE

We are the music-makers,
    And we are the dreamers of dreams,
Wandering by lone sea-breakers,
    And sitting by desolate streams —
World-losers and world-forsakers,
    On whom the pale moon gleams:
Yet we are the movers and shakers
    Of the world for ever, it seems.

We, in the ages lying
    In the buried past of the earth,
Built Nineveh with our sighing,
    And Babel itself with our mirth;
And o'erthrew them with prophesying
    To the old of the new world's worth;
For each age is a dream that is dying,
    Or one that is coming to birth.

ARTHUR O'SHAUGHNESSY

THE LAMPLIGHTER

Here to the leisured side of life,
Remote from traffic, free from strife,
A cul-de-sac, a sanctuary
Where old quaint customs creep to die
And only ancient memories stir,
At evening comes the lamplighter;
With measured steps, without a sound,
He treads the unalterable round,
Soundlessly touching one by one
The waiting posts that stand to take
And when the night begins to wane
He comes to take them back again,
Before the chilly dawn can blight
The delicate frail buds of light.

SEUMAS O'SULLIVAN

A PIPER

A piper in the street today,
Set up, and tuned, and started to play,
And away, away, away on the tide
Of his music we started; on every side
Doors and windows were opened wide,
And men left down their work and came,
And women with petticoats coloured like flame,
And little bare feet that were blue with cold,
Went dancing back to the age of gold,
And all the world went gay, went gay,
For half an hour in the street today.

SEUMAS O'SULLIVAN

THE MOTHER

I do not grudge them: Lord, I do not grudge
My two strong sons that I have seen go out
To break their strength and die, they and a few,
In bloody protest for a glorious thing,
They shall be spoken of among their people,
The generations shall remember them,
And call them blessed;
But I will speak their names to my own heart
In the long nights;
The little names that were familiar once
Round my dead hearth.
Lord, thou art hard on mothers;
We suffer in their coming and their going;
And tho' I grudge them not, I weary, weary
Of the long sorrow — And yet I have my joy:
My sons were faithful, and they fought.

PATRICK PEARSE

THE BELLS OF SHANDON

With deep affection and recollection
  I often think of the Shandon bells,
Whose sounds so wild would, in days of childhood,
  Fling round my cradle their magic spells.
On this I ponder, where'er I wander,
  And thus grow fonder, sweet Cork, of thee;
      With thy bells of Shandon,
      That sound so grand on
  The pleasant waters of the river Lee.

I have heard bells chiming full many a clime in,
  Tolling sublime in cathedral shrine;
While at a glib rate brass tongues would vibrate,
  But all their music spoke nought to thine;
For memory dwelling on each proud swelling
  Of thy belfry knelling its bold notes free,
      Made the bells of Shandon
      Sound far more grand on
  The pleasant waters of the river Lee.

I have heard bells tolling 'old Adrian's mole' in,
  Their thunder rolling from the Vatican,
With cymbals glorious, swinging uproarious
  In the gorgeous turrets of Notre Dame;
But thy sounds were sweeter than the dome of Peter
  Flings o'er the Tiber, pealing solemnly.
      Oh! the bells of Shandon
      Sound far more grand on
  The pleasant waters of the river Lee.

There's a bell in Moscow, while on tower and Kiosko
  In St Sophia the Turkman gets,
And loud in air calls men to prayer
  From the tapering summit of tall minarets.
Such empty phantom I freely grant 'em,

But there's an anthem more dear to me:
    'Tis the bells of Shandon,
    That sound so grand on
The pleasant waters of the river Lee.

FATHER PROUT
(Francis Sylvester Mahony)

I AM RAIFTEIRÍ

I am Raifteirí, the poet, full of courage and love,
my eyes without light, in calmness serene,
taking my way by the light of my heart
feeble and tired to the end of the road:
look at me now, my face toward Balla,
playing my music to empty pockets!

ANTOINE RAIFTEIRÍ
translated by Thomas Kinsella

HOME THOUGHTS FROM ABROAD

Hearing, this June day, the thin thunder
Of far-off invective and old denunciation
Lambasting and lambegging the homeland,
I think of that brave man Paisley, eyeless
In Gaza, with a daisy-chain of millstones
Round his neck; groping, like blind Samson,
for the soapy pillars and greased poles of lightning
To pull them down in rains and borborygmic roars
Of rhetoric. (There but for the grace of God
Goes God.) I like his people and I like his guts
But I dislike his gods who always end
In gun-play. Some day, of course, he'll be one
With the old giants of Ireland — such as
Denis of the Drought, or Iron-Buttocks —
Who had at last to be reduced to size,
Quietly shrunken into 'wee people'
And put out to grass on the hills for good,
Minimized like cars or skirts or mums;
Photostatted to fit a literate age
And filed safely away on the dark shelves
Of memory; preserved in ink, oak-gall,
Alcohol, aspic, piety, wit. A pity,
Perhaps, if it is drama one wants. But,
Look at it this way: in this day and age
We can't really have giants lumbering
All over the place, cluttering it up,
With hair like ropes, flutes like telegraph poles,
And feet like tramcars, intent only on dogging
The fled horse of history and the Boyne.
So today across the Irish Sea I wave
And wish him well from the bottom of my heart
Where truth lies bleeding, its ear-drums burst
By the blather of his hand-me-down talk.
In fond memory of his last stand
I dedicate this contraceptive pill

Of poetry to his unborn followers,
And I place
This bucket of beget-me-nots on his grave.

W. R. RODGERS

LET THE TOAST PASS

Here's to the maiden of bashful fifteen,
   Here's to the widow of fifty,
Here's to the flaunting extravagant quean,
   And here's to the housewife that's thrifty.
      Let the toast pass, Drink to the lass,
      I'll warrant she'll prove an excuse for the glass.

Here's to the charmer whose dimples we prize,
   Here's to the maid who has none, sir;
Here's to the girl with a pair of blue eyes,
   And here's to the nymph with but one, sir.
      Let the toast pass, etc.

Here's to the maid with a bosom of snow,
   And to her that's as brown as a berry;
Here's to the wife with a face full of woe,
   And now to the girl that is merry.
      Let the toast pass, etc.

For let 'em be clumsy, or let 'em be slim,
   Young or ancient, I care not a feather;
So fill the pint bumpers quite up to the brim,
   And let us e'en toast 'em together.
      Let the toast pass, Drink to the lass,
      I'll warrant she'll prove an excuse for the glass.

RICHARD BRINSLEY SHERIDAN

THE SHELL

And then I pressed the shell
Close to my ear
And listened well,
And straightway like a bell
Came low and clear
The slow, sad murmur of far distant seas,
Whipped by an icy breeze
Upon a shore
Wind-swept and desolate.
It was a sunless strand that never bore
The footprint of a man,
Nor felt the weight
Since time began
Of any human quality or stir
Save what the dreary winds and waves incur.
And in the hush of waters was the sound
Of pebbles rolling round,
For ever rolling with a hollow sound.
And bubbling sea-weeds as the waters go
Swish to and fro
Their long, cold tentacles of slimy grey.
There was no day,
Nor ever came a night
Setting the stars alight
To wonder at the moon:
Was twilight only and the frightened croon,
Smitten to whimpers, of the dreary wind
And waves that journeyed blind –
And then I loosed my ear – oh, it was sweet
To hear a cart go jolting down the street!

JAMES STEPHENS

A GLASS OF BEER

The lanky hank of a she in the inn over there
Nearly killed me for asking the loan of a glass of beer;
May the devil grip the whey-faced slut by the hair,
And beat bad manners out of her skin for a year.

That parboiled ape, with the toughest jaw you will see
On virtue's path, and a voice that would rasp the dead,
Came roaring and raging the minute she looked at me,
And threw me out of the house on the back of my head!

If I asked her master he'd give me a cask a day;
But she, with the beer at hand, not a gill would arrange!
May she marry a ghost and bear him a kitten, and may
The High King of Glory permit her to get the mange.

JAMES STEPHENS

SONG FROM THE BACKWOODS

Deep in Canadian woods we've met,
    From one bright island flown;
Great is the land we tread, but yet
    Our hearts are with our own,
And ere we leave this shanty small,
    While fades the autumn day,
    We'll toast Old Ireland!
    Dear Old Ireland!
    Ireland, boys, Hurrah!

We've heard her faults a hundred times,
    The new ones and the old,
In songs and sermons, rants and rhymes,
    Enlarged some fifty-fold.
But take them all, the great and small,
    And this we've got to say:
    Here's dear Old Ireland!
    Good Old Ireland!
    Ireland, boys, Hurrah!

We know that brave and good men tried
    To snap her rusty chain —
That patriots suffered, martyrs died,
    And all, 'tis said, in vain:
But no, boys, no! a glance will show
    How far they've won their way —
    Here's good Old Ireland!
    Loved Old Ireland!
    Ireland, boys, Hurrah!

We've seen the wedding and the wake,
    The patron and the fair;
And lithe young frames at the dear old games
    In the kindly Irish air;
With a loud 'hurroo' and a 'pillalu,'

And the thundering 'Clear the way!' —
Here's gay Old Ireland!
Dear Old Ireland!
Ireland, boys, Hurrah!

And well we know in the cool grey eves,
    When the hard day's work is o'er,
How soft and sweet are the words that greet
    The friends that meet once more;
With 'Mary machree!' and 'My Pat! 'tis he!'
    And 'My own heart night and day!'
    Ah, fond Old Ireland!
    Dear Old Ireland!
    Ireland, boys, Hurrah!

And happy and bright are the groups that pass,
    From their peaceful homes, for miles
O'er fields, and roads, and hills, to Mass,
    When Sunday morning smiles!
And deep the zeal their true hearts feel
    When low they kneel and pray.
    Oh, Dear Old Ireland!
    Blest Old Ireland!
    Ireland, boys, Hurrah!

But deep in Canadian woods we've met,
    And we never shall see again
The dear old isle where our hearts are set,
    And our first fond hopes remain!
But come, fill up another cup,
    And with every sup let's say —
    Here's loved old Ireland!
    Good Old Ireland!
    Ireland, boys, Hurrah!

TIMOTHY DANIEL SULLIVAN

All travellers at first incline
Where'er they see the fairest sign,
And if they find the chambers neat,
And like the liquor and the meat,
Will call again, and recommend
The Angel Inn to every friend.
And though the painting grows decay'd,
The house will never lose its trade:
Nay, though the treach'rous tapster, Thomas,
Hangs a new Angel two doors from us,
As fine as daubers' hands can make it,
In hopes that strangers may mistake it,
We think it both a shame and sin
To quit the true old Angel Inn.
   Now this is Stella's case in fact,
An angel's face a little crack'd.
(Could poets or could painters fix
How angels look at thirty-six:)
This drew us in at first to find
In such a form an angel's mind;
And every virtue now supplies
The fainting rays of Stella's eyes.
See, at her levee crowding swains,
Whom Stella freely entertains
With breeding, humour, wit, and sense,
And puts them to so small expense;
Their minds so plentifully fills,
And makes such reasonable bills,
So little gets for what she gives,
We really wonder how she lives!
And had her stock been less, no doubt
She must have long ago run out.
   Then, who can think we'll quit the place,
When Doll hangs out a newer face?
Nail'd to her window full in sight

All Christian people to invite,
Or stop and light at Chloe's head,
With scraps and leavings to be fed?
   Then, Chloe, still go on to prate
Of thirty-six and thirty-eight;
Pursue your trade of scandal-picking,
Your hints that Stella is no chicken;
Your innuendoes, when you tell us,
That Stella loves to talk with fellows:
But let me warn you to believe
A truth, for which your soul should grieve;
That should you live to see the day,
When Stella's locks must all be gray,
When age must print a furrow'd trace
On every feature of her face;
Though you, and all your senseless tribe,
Could Art, or Time, or Nature bribe,
To make you look like Beauty's Queen,
And hold for ever at fifteen;
No bloom of youth can ever blind
The cracks and wrinkles of your mind:
All men of sense will pass your door,
And crowd to Stella's at four-score.

JONATHAN SWIFT

SHEEP AND LAMBS

All in the April evening,
    April airs were abroad,
The sheep with their little lambs
    Passed me by on the road.

The sheep with their little lambs
    Passed me by on the road;
All in the April evening
    I thought on the Lamb of God.

The lambs were weary, and crying
    With a weak, human cry.
I thought on the Lamb of God
    Going meekly to die.

Up in the blue, blue mountains
    Dewy pastures are sweet;
Rest for the little bodies,
    Rest for the little feet,

But for the Lamb of God,
    Up on the hilltop green,
Only a cross of shame
    Two stark crosses between.

All in the April evening,
    April airs were abroad;
I saw the sheep with their lambs,
    And thought on the Lamb of God.

KATHARINE TYNAN

LARKS

All day in exquisite air
The song clomb an invisible stair,
Flight on flight, story on story,
Into the dazzling glory.

There was no bird, only a singing,
Up in the glory, climbing and ringing,
Like a small golden cloud at even,
Trembling 'twixt earth and heaven.

I saw no staircase winding, winding,
Up in the dazzle, sapphire and blinding,
Yet round by round, in exquisite air,
The song went up the stair.

KATHARINE TYNAN

REQUIESCAT

Tread light, she is near
Under the snow,
Speak gently, she can hear
The daisies grow.

All her bright golden hair
Tarnished with rust,
She that was young and fair
Fallen to dust.

Lily-like, white as snow,
She hardly knew
She was a woman, so
Sweetly she grew.

Coffin-board, heavy stone
Lie on her breast,
I vex my heart alone,
She is at rest.

Peace, Peace, she cannot hear
Lyre or sonnet,
All my life's buried here,
Heap earth upon it.

OSCAR WILDE

from THE BALLAD OF READING GAOL

He did not wear his scarlet coat,
    For blood and wine are red,
And blood and wine were on his hands
    When they found him with the dead,
The poor dead woman whom he loved,
    And murdered in her bed.

He walked amongst the Trial Men
    In a suit of shabby grey;
A cricket cap was on his head,
    And his step seemed light and gay;
But I never saw a man who looked
    So wistfully at the day.

I never saw a man who looked
    With such a wistful eye
Upon that little tent of blue
    Which prisoners call the sky,
And at every drifting cloud that went
    With sails of silver by.

I walked, with other souls in pain,
    Within another ring,
And was wondering if the man had done
    A great or little thing,
When a voice behind me whispered low,
    'That fellow's got to swing.'

OSCAR WILDE

LES SILHOUETTES

The sea is flecked with bars of grey,
   The dull dead wind is out of tune,
   And like a withered leaf the moon
Is blown across the stormy bay.

Etched clear upon the pallid sand
   Lies the black boat: a sailor boy
   Clambers aboard in careless joy
With laughing face and gleaming hand.

And overhead the curlews cry,
   Where through the dusky upland grass
   The young brown-throated reapers pass,
Like silhouettes against the sky.

OSCAR WILDE

THE DYING GIRL

From a Munster vale they brought her,
  From the pure and balmy air;
An Ormond peasant's daughter,
  With blue eyes and golden hair.
They brought her to the city,
  And she faded slowly there —
Consumption has no pity
  For blue eyes and golden hair.

When I saw her first reclining,
  Her lips were mov'd in prayer,
And the setting sun was shining
  On her loosen'd golden hair.
When our kindly glances met her,
  Deadly brilliant was her eye;
And she said that she was better,
  While we knew that she must die.

She speaks of Munster valleys,
  The pattern, dance, and fair,
And her thin hand feebly dallies
  With her scattered golden hair.
When silently we listen'd
  To her breath with quiet care,
Her eyes with wonder glisten'd,
  And she asked us, 'What was there?'

The poor thing smiled to ask it,
  And her pretty mouth laid bare,
Like gems within a casket,
  A string of pearlets rare.
We said that we were trying
  By the gushing of her blood
And the time she took in sighing
  To know if she were good.

136

Well, she smil'd and chatted gaily,
    Though we saw in mute despair
The hectic brighter daily,
    And the death-dew on her hair.
And oft her wasted fingers
    Beating time upon the bed:
O'er some old tune she lingers,
    And she bows her golden head.

At length the harp is broken;
    And the spirit in its strings,
As the last decree is spoken,
    To its source exulting springs.
Descending swiftly from the skies
    Her guardian angel came,
He struck God's lightning from her eyes,
    And bore Him back the flame.

Before the sun had risen
    Through the lark-loved morning air,
Her young soul left its prison,
    Undefiled by sin or care.
I stood beside the couch in tears
    Where pale and calm she slept,
And though I've gaz'd on death for years,
    I blush not that I wept.

I check'd with effort pity's sighs
    And left the matron there,
To close the curtains of her eyes
    And bind her golden hair.

RICHARD DALTON WILLIAMS

137

THE MAN FROM GOD-KNOWS-WHERE

Into our townlan', on a night of snow,
Rode a man from God-knows-where;
None of us bade him stay or go,
Nor deemed him friend, nor damned him foe.
But we stabled his big roan mare;
For in our townlan' we're decent folk,
And if he didn't speak, why none of us spoke,
And we sat till the fire burned low.

We're a civil sort in our wee place
So we made the circle wide
Round Andy Lemon's cheerful blaze,
And wished the man his length of days,
And a good end to his ride.
He smiled in under his slouchy hat —
Says he: 'There's a bit of a joke in that,
For we ride different ways.'

The whiles we smoked we watched him stare
From his seat fornenst the glow.
I nudged Joe Moore: 'You wouldn't dare
To ask him, who he's for meeting there,
And how far he has got to go.'
And Joe wouldn't dare, nor Wully Scott,
And he took no drink — neither cold nor hot —
This man from God-knows-where.

It was closin' time, an' late forbye,
When us ones braved the air —
I never saw worse (may I live or die)
Than the sleet that night, an' I says, says I:
'You'll find he's for stopping there.'
But at screek o' day, through the gable pane,
I watched him spur in the peltin' rain,
And I juked from his rovin' eye.

Two winters more, then the Trouble Year,
When the best that a man can feel
Was the pike he kept in hidin's near,
Till the blood o' hate an' the blood o' fear
Would be redder nor rust on the steel.
Us ones quet from mindin' the farms,
Let them take what we gave wi' the weight o' our arms
From Saintfield to Kilkeel.

In the time o' the Hurry, we had no lead —
We all of us fought with the rest —
An' if e'er a one shook like a tremblin' reed,
None of us gave neither hint nor heed.
Nor ever even'd we'd guessed.
We men of the North had a word to say,
An' we said it then, in our own dour way,
An' we spoke as we thought was best.

All Ulster over, the weemen cried
For the stan'in' crops on the lan' —
Many's the sweetheart an' many's the bride
Would liefer ha' gone till where He died,
And ha' mourned her lone by her man.
But us ones weathered the thick of it,
And we used to dander along and sit,
In Andy's, side by side.

What with discorse goin' to and fro,
The night would be wearin' thin,
Yet never so late when we rose to go
But someone would say: 'Do ye min' thon snow,
An' the man who came wanderin' in?'
And we be to fall to the talk again,
If by any chance he was One o' Them —
The man who went like the win'.

Well 'twas gettin' on past the heat o' the year
When I rode to Newtown fair;
I sold as I could (the dealers were near –
Only three pounds eight for the Innish steer,
An' nothin' at all for the mare!)
I met M'Kee in the throng o' the street,
Says he: 'The grass has grown under our feet
Since they hanged young Warwick here.'

And he told me that Boney had promised help
To a man in Dublin town.
Says he: 'If you've laid the pike on the shelf,
Ye'd better go home hot-fut by yourself,
An' once more take it down.'
So by Comber road I trotted the grey
And never cut corn until Killyleagh
Stood plain on the rising groun'.

For a wheen o' days we sat waitin' the word
To rise and go at it like men.
But no French ships sailed into Cloughey Bay,
And we heard the black news on a harvest day
That the cause was lost again;
And Joey and me, and Wully Boy Scott,
We agreed to ourselves we'd as lief as not
Ha' been found in the thick o' the slain.

By Downpatrick gaol I was bound to fare
On a day I'll remember, feth,
For when I came to the prison square
The people were waitin' in hundreds there,
An' you wouldn't hear stir nor breath!
For the sodgers were standing, grim an' tall,
Round a scaffold built there fornent the wall,
An' a man stepped out for death!

I was brave an' near to the edge of the throng,
Yet I knowed the face again.
An' I knowed the set, an' I knowed the walk
An' the sound of his strange up-country talk,
For he spoke out right an' plain.
Then he bowed his head to the swinging rope,
Whiles I said, 'Please God' to his dying hope,
And 'Amen' to his dying prayer,
That the Wrong would cease and the Right prevail,
For the man that they hanged at Downpatrick gaol
Was the Man from GOD-KNOWS-WHERE!

FLORENCE M. WILSON

THE BURIAL OF SIR JOHN MOORE

Not a drum was heard, not a funeral note,
  As his corse to the ramparts we hurried;
Not a soldier discharged his farewell shot
  O'er the grave where our hero we buried.

We buried him darkly, at dead of night,
  The sods with our bayonets turning,
By the struggling moonbeam's misty light,
  And the lantern dimly burning.

No useless coffin enclosed his breast,
  Not in sheet nor in shroud we wound him;
But he lay like a warrior taking his rest,
  With his martial cloak around him.

Few and short were the prayers we said,
  And we spake not a word of sorrow;
But we steadfastly gazed on the face that was dead,
  And we bitterly thought of the morrow.

We thought as we hollowed his narrow bed,
  And smoothed down his lonely pillow,
That the foe and the stranger would tread o'er his head,
  And we far away on the billow!

Lightly they'll talk of the spirit that's gone,
  And o'er his cold ashes upbraid him –
But little he'll reck if they let him sleep on
  In a grave where a Briton has laid him.

But half of our heavy task was done,
  When the clock struck the hour for retiring,
And we heard the distant and random gun
  That the foe was sullenly firing.

Slowly and sadly we laid him down,
    From the field of his fame fresh and gory;
We carved not a line, and we raised not a stone —
    But we left him alone in his glory!

CHARLES WOLFE

EASTER 1916

I have met them at close of day
Coming with vivid faces
From counter or desk among grey
Eighteenth-century houses.
I have passed with a nod of the head
Or polite meaningless words,
Or have lingered awhile and said
Polite meaningless words,
And thought before I had done
Of a mocking tale or a gibe
To please a companion
Around the fire at the club,
Being certain that they and I
But lived where motley is worn:
All changed, changed utterly:
A terrible beauty is born.

That woman's days were spent
In ignorant good-will,
Her nights in argument
Until her voice grew shrill.
What voice more sweet than hers
When, young and beautiful,
She rode to harriers?
This man had kept a school
And rode our wingèd horse;
This other his helper and friend
Was coming into his force;
He might have won fame in the end,
So sensitive his nature seemed,
So daring and sweet his thought.
This other man I had dreamed
A drunken, vainglorious lout.
He had done most bitter wrong
To some who are near my heart,

Yet I number him in the song;
He, too, has resigned his part
In the casual comedy;
He, too, has been changed in his turn,
Transformed utterly:
A terrible beauty is born.

Hearts with one purpose alone
Through summer and winter seem
Enchanted to a stone
To trouble the living stream.
The horse that comes from the road,
The rider, the birds that range
From cloud to tumbling cloud,
Minute by minute they change;
A shadow of cloud on the stream
Changes minute by minute;
A horse-hoof slides on the brim,
And a horse plashes within it;
The long-legged moor-hens dive,
And hens to moor-cocks call;
Minute by minute they live:
The stone's in the midst of all.

Too long a sacrifice
Can make a stone of the heart.
O when may it suffice?
That is Heaven's part, our part
To murmur name upon name,
As a mother names her child
When sleep at last has come
On limbs that had run wild.
What is it but nightfall?
No, no, not night but death;
Was it needless death after all?

For England may keep faith
For all that is done and said.
We know their dream; enough
To know they dreamed and are dead;
And what if excess of love
Bewildered them till they died?
I write it out in a verse —
MacDonagh and MacBride
And Connolly and Pearse
Now and in time to be,
Wherever green is worn,
Are changed, changed utterly:
A terrible beauty is born.

WILLIAM BUTLER YEATS

DOWN BY THE SALLEY GARDENS

Down by the salley gardens my love and I did meet;
She passed the salley gardens with little snow-white feet.
She bid me take love easy, as the leaves grow on the tree;
But I, being young and foolish, with her would not agree.

In a field by the river my love and I did stand,
And on my leaning shoulder she laid her snow-white hand.
She bid me take life easy, as the grass grows on the weirs;
But I was young and foolish, and now am full of tears.

WILLIAM BUTLER YEATS

WHEN YOU ARE OLD

When you are old and grey and full of sleep,
   And nodding by the fire, take down this book,
   And slowly read, and dream of the soft look
Your eyes had once, and of their shadows deep:

How many loved your moments of glad grace,
   And loved your beauty with love false or true!
   But one man loved the pilgrim soul in you,
And loved the sorrows of your changing face.

And bending down beside the glowing bars
   Murmur, a little sadly, how love fled
   And paced upon the mountains overhead
And hid his face amid a crowd of stars.

WILLIAM BUTLER YEATS

THE BALLAD OF FATHER GILLIGAN

The old priest Peter Gilligan
  Was weary night and day;
For half his flock were in their beds,
  Or under green sods lay.

Once, while he nodded on a chair,
  At the moth-hour of eve,
Another poor man sent for him,
  And be began to grieve.

'I have no rest, nor joy, nor peace,
  For people die and die;'
And after cried he, 'God forgive!
  My body spake, not I!'

He knelt, and leaning on the chair
  He prayed and fell asleep;
And the moth-hour went from the fields,
  And stars began to peep.

They slowly into millions grew,
  And leaves shook in the wind;
And God covered the world with shade,
  And whispered to mankind.

Upon the time of sparrow chirp
  When the moths came once more,
The old priest Peter Gilligan
  Stood upright on the floor.

'*Mavrone, mavrone!* the man has died,
  While I slept on the chair;'
He roused his horse out of its sleep,
  And rode with little care.

He rode now as he never rode,
   By rocky lane and fen;
The sick man's wife opened the door:
   'Father! you come again!'

'And is the poor man dead?' he cried.
   'He died an hour ago,'
The old priest Peter Gilligan
   In grief swayed to and fro.

'When you were gone, he turned and died
   As merry as a bird.'
The old priest Peter Gilligan
   He knelt him at that word.

'He who hath made the night of stars
   For souls, who tire and bleed,
Sent one of His great angels down
   To help me in my need.

'He who is wrapped in purple robes,
   With planets in His care,
Had pity on the least of things
   Asleep upon a chair.'

WILLIAM BUTLER YEATS

ACKNOWLEDGEMENTS

Grateful acknowledgement is made to:

Campbell Thomson & McLaughlin Ltd for permission to reprint 'Home Thoughts from Abroad' by W.R. Rodgers;

The estate of the late Padraic Colum for permission to reprint 'A Drover', 'An Old Woman of the Roads' and 'She Moved Through the Fair';

Maurice James Craig for permission to reprint 'Ballad to a Traditional Refrain';

Devin-Adair Publishers for permission to reprint 'Ringsend' and 'Golden Stockings' by Oliver St John Gogarty;

Faber & Faber Ltd for permission to reprint 'The Meeting Point' by Louis MacNeice from *The Collected Poems of Louis MacNeice*;

Peter Fallon on behalf of Katherine Kavanagh for permission to reprint 'A Christmas Childhood', 'Epic' and 'Shancoduff' by Patrick Kavanagh;

Allen Figgis & Co. for permission to reprint 'My Lagan Love' by Joseph Campbell;

Molly Keane for permission to reprint 'Corrymeela' by Moira O'Neill;

Brendan Kennelly for permission to reprint 'My Story';

Thomas Kinsella for permission to reprint 'Valentine Browne', 'I am Raifteirí', 'Keep Your Kiss to Yourself' and 'The Scholar's Life';

John Montague for permission to reprint 'The Son of the King of Moy', 'The Vikings' and 'Belfast Lough';

Oxford University Press for permission to reprint 'The Student and his Cat' from *The Irish Tradition* (1947) by Robin Flower;

A.D. Peters & Co. Ltd for permission to reprint 'The Midnight Court' (extract), 'On the Death of his Wife', 'The Lament for Art O'Leary' (extract), 'The Hermit's Song' and 'Kilcash' by Frank O'Connor;

Joan Rea for permission to reprint 'The Man from God-knows-where' by Florence M. Wilson;

Martin Secker & Warburg Ltd for permission to reprint 'The Widow of Drynam' by Patrick MacDonogh;

The Society of Authors on behalf of the copyright owner, Mrs Iris Wise, for permission to reprint 'A Glass of Beer' and 'The Shell' by James Stephens;

A.P. Watt Ltd for permission to reprint 'Easter 1916', 'When You are Old', 'Down by the Salley Gardens', 'The Ballad of Father Gilligan' and 'The Song of Wandering Aengus' (extract) by W.B. Yeats.

The publishers have made every effort to trace and acknowledge copyright holders. We apologise for any omissions in the above list and we will welcome additions or amendments to it for inclusion in any reprint edition.

INDEX OF TITLES AND FIRST LINES